P9-APU-906

The Q Guide to

Will & Grace

The Q Guides

FROM ALYSON BOOKS

AVAILABLE NOW:

POP CULTURE

Q

OUT THERE

GUIDE

The Q Guide to

Will & Grace

**Stuff You Didn't Even Know You Wanted
to Know . . .** about Will, Grace, Jack,
Karen, and lots of guest stars

[Corinne Marshall]

alyson books
NEW YORK

CORRESPONDENCE ON PAGES 22–23 REPRINTED
WITH THE PERMISSION OF JON KINNALLY.

MANUFACTURED IN THE UNITED STATES OF AMERICA

A TRADE PAPERBACK ORIGINAL
PUBLISHED BY ALYSON BOOKS
245 WEST 17TH STREET,
NEW YORK, NY 10011

DISTRIBUTION IN THE UNITED KINGDOM BY
TURNAROUND PUBLISHER SERVICES LTD.
UNIT 3, OLYMPIA TRADING ESTATE
COBURG ROAD, WOOD GREEN
LONDON N22 6TZ ENGLAND

FIRST EDITION: AUGUST 2008

08 09 10 11 12 13 14 15 16 17 a 10 9 8 7 6 5 4 3 2 1

ISBN-10: 1-59350-083-1
ISBN-13: 978-1-59350-083-2

LIBRARY OF CONGRESS CATALOGING-IN-PUBLICATION DATA
ARE ON FILE.

COVER DESIGN BY VICTOR MINGOVITS
COVER ART BY www.glenhanson.com

This book is dedicated to Janis Hirsch
for being a wonderful mentor, friend, and inspiration.

Contents

Introduction

FOR A JEWISH GIRL born and raised on the corner of tranny and show tune, otherwise known as Manhattan's West Fifties, finding a gay husband was as much a rite of passage as learning to hail a cab. Being a fag hag, a fruit fly, a queen bee, or simply a gay wife was an expectation, not an aspiration. At some point in the future, you just knew you'd find that man to walk down the aisle of a shoe store with.

By the nineties, the relationship with girls and their gays was not only becoming a cultural norm, but one only had to look to the movies to see the appeal of such a union: Girl friends were *Single White Female.* Gay men were *My Best Friend's Wedding.*

When *Will & Grace* came along in 1998, I realized I had never really seen that dynamic on television before. And I had definitely never seen a gay leading man or a Jewish woman who wasn't obsessed with landing a husband (I'm looking at you, Nanny Fine). The characters were unique for the small screen, but we (and by "we" I mean mostly urban dwellers or patrons of the arts or people living in neighborhoods on the cusp of gentrification or theater folk, etc., etc.) *knew* those people. Jack McFarland, with his whirling dervish wrist flips, may have been a stereotype, but that guy exists. I'm friends with five of him.

Will & Grace was a cultural milestone and a consistently hysterical sitcom—no small feat in an era where "fat man with skinny wife" was devouring the genre with burps and bon mots as fresh as an Arby's sub. But what I loved most about the show was that at its heart, it was about a beautiful friendship.

—Corinne Marshall, March 2008

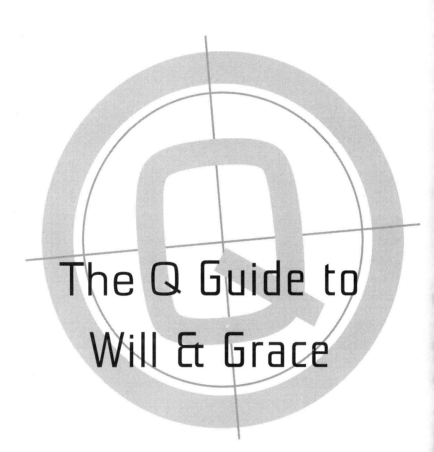

The Q Guide to
Will & Grace

The Early Days

> "It's a gay network, for God's sake! The symbol is a peacock!"
>
> —Jack McFarland, on NBC

Will and Grace: That Couple Next Door

It's 1997, and NBC is looking for the next *Mad About You*. The romantic comedy starring Paul Reiser and Helen Hunt is about to go gently into sitcom history, and the network needs a new couple to entertain America. Scribes Max Mutchnick and David Kohan, friends since their days at Beverly Hills High School, have a development deal with the Peacock and are called upon to create the new romance. Luckily David, who had worked as Sydney Pollack's assistant, receives invaluable advice from the Hollywood legend: (1) "A love story is over when the boy and girl kiss," (2) "A love story is only as good as the obstacles you throw at it."

Q FACT

The names Will and Grace were inspired by a passage from the Jewish theologian Martin Buber's, *I-Thou*, which states: "You need the *will* to pursue a relationship with God, and the *grace* to receive it."

For their first attempt at a new series, Max and David cook up the perfect love story with obstacles galore and a boy and girl who will never share a kiss (as lovers, anyway). The only catch is that these "lovebirds" live down the hall from the main characters. The show that Max and David create is about three San Francisco couples: one married, one on the verge, and their next-door neighbors, some gay man and his straight-gal roomie: Will and Grace.

David recalls that during a meeting with David Nevins, NBC's Senior Vice President of Primetime Series at the time, and Warren Littlefield, the network's former entertainment president, David and Max gave "dissertations" on Will and Grace but were relatively silent when it came to their other characters. The network bigwigs felt the writers had more of a handle on that duo and wanted them to write another show focusing on them. But Max and David had their doubts about doing a show with a gay leading man. Max, an openly gay man, felt uneasy about what "NBC would say about the subject," he says in his commentary on the Season 1 DVD. At the time, in sitcoms gay characters never occupied leading roles. They were funny neighbors, sidekicks, guest stars—mostly men who would drop in, toss out a biting bon mot, and swish off camera. The one exception, *Ellen*, the ABC sitcom starring Ellen DeGeneres, saw its ratings drop dramatically after Ellen's character came out.

Although *Ellen*'s ratings were circling the drain, mainstream America was warming to the idea of straight women and gay men as friends. *My Best Friend's Wedding* had recently been in theaters "and everyone was responding" to the friendship between Julia Roberts's straight woman and Rupert Everett's gay man, says David. The straight woman/gay man relationship was "kind of ubiquitous," he adds. And, as it turned out, Max had a lot of experience with that particular dynamic: Before there was Will and Grace, there was Max and Janet Eisenberg, Max's high school girlfriend.

Max and Janet

Max, Janet, and David were good friends and eager participants in the Beverly Hills High School drama department. While Max was at Emerson University in Boston, he came out as a gay man, but as far as Janet knew, he was still "the one." Over the years, David and Max would get together for writing sessions and try their hand at collaboration. During one of these sessions, Max told David he was gay, making David the first straight man he ever told. David "kind of knew" already, and the revelation didn't have any effect on their friendship. Janet, on the other hand, was devastated.

David says girlfriends are like mothers in that "they are the first to know and the last to find out." He believes Janet "knew but she didn't know." For the next year, Janet wouldn't speak to Max, and David acted as their liaison. "The Henry Kissinger of love," he says. Like Will and Grace, Max and Janet eventually resumed their friendship.

While the two were pondering stories for a romantic comedy with an insurmountable obstacle, David said to Max: "You and Janet."

Jimmy Burrows: The High Priest of Sitcoms

Before going ahead with the show, Littlefield wanted Max and David to meet with legendary sitcom director James Burrows, a name that has appeared across the screen of countless classic sitcoms, including *The Mary Tyler Moore Show, Rhoda, Taxi, Cheers, Frasier,* and *Friends.*

"Jimmy was the high priest of sitcoms," says David. "If he deemed to do one of your scripts as a pilot you should be honored, but our attitude was, 'he's the 800-pound gorilla and this was our baby.' We didn't want someone else making it his." Max and David planned to meet with James, say, "thanks but no thanks," and move on. Their plans changed when they came face to face with the legend. "We sit down next to him and we're like, 'That's Jimmy Burrows, that name we see on TV a lot.' Jimmy said, 'I read the script and I think I want to do it' and we both say, 'Great!'"

James felt the rooting interest of *Will & Grace* was to see Will and Grace together. "But it's a tease because it will never happen," says David. "Will will never not be gay."

Casting *Will & Grace*: 1 Canadian, 1 Bottle of Vodka, 1 Traffic Ticket, and Sean Hayes's Ass

QUOTE

"They were worried we'd end up with Paul Lynde."

—Series Co-Creator David Kohan, on casting Will

Tracy Lilienfield, the show's casting director, recalls the four main actors, Eric McCormack, Debra Messing, Megan Mullally, and Sean Hayes, all initially turning down their roles. "We adored them," she says. "But there was a period of time when we didn't think we could get them."

For the network, Will was the most difficult role to cast. Don Ohlmeyer, the president of the West Coast division of NBC at the time, was especially nervous. The actor who would play Will had to be a leading man who was funny and capable of playing a gay character without going camp. For David, Eric, with his Canuck roots and leading man background, was a natural choice as Will. "Being gay and being a Canadian thespian are so close. Such a fine line," he says wryly.

When Eric McCormack auditioned, everyone agreed that he was Will . . . except for Eric. "Eric auditioned and everyone liked him," says David, "but he got cold feet." Eric was worried that if the show succeeded, he would be Will Truman for the rest of his career and if the show failed, he would be the face of a failed sitcom. "If you're in a sitcom that works, you're identified like that forever," says David. "On a sitcom, you're in people's homes, in the cultural fabric. Eric was worried that it would cost him down the road." After Eric turned down Will, Max said to him, "We understand. Go think about it."

Eric had the holiday break to think it over. During that time, he reread the script, and thought about the part of Will Truman more from an actor's perspective than from that of a rising star. His conclusion: "Why wouldn't I do this?"

Now that there was a Will, there needed to be a Grace. Debra Messing, a Jewish girl born in Brooklyn, raised in Rhode Island, and gifted with expert comic timing seemed perfect. She was "the kind of girl you could've gone to camp with," says David. But at first, Debra was unavailable, shooting the television drama *Prey*. After *Prey* ended, Debra wanted to take a break, says David. "She wanted to go to New York and do theater." To convince Debra to consider the part, Max and David showed up at her apartment with a bottle of vodka and a lime. By the end of the night, Debra agreed to read for the role of Grace.

While Max and David saw Debra Messing as Grace, the network still wanted them to look at two other actresses, one of whom was Nicolette Sheridan, who later guest-starred as the hot-for-Grace's-hubby, Dr. Morty. The writers told the actresses that no one else was being considered for the role of Grace Adler. "Each woman was told she was the only one auditioning at Jimmy's house. We got them all cars and staggered them, so no one could see the others coming," says David.

During her reading with Eric McCormack, everyone in the room knew they were watching two best friends: Will and Grace. "Debra came and the two of them together were so good. It was so exciting," recalls David. James agrees. "When Debra read with Eric, there was no doubt," he says. Eric McCormack also knew that he and Debra clicked. Over a month he read with a lot of actresses, but when he read with Debra he thought, "Oh, thank God." Says Eric on the DVD commentary for Season 1, "It was only when Debra came in. She laughed at [Will's] jokes," like a real friend would.

Casting Karen and Jack presented other problems. Both Sean Hayes and Megan Mullally wanted to play the leads, not the drama queen sidekick and the leading lady's pill-popping assistant. Megan says in her commentary on the Season 1 DVD: "I auditioned for Grace. Big flatline. I didn't want to read for Karen for a variety of imbecilic reasons." Luckily Megan changed her mind. She was driving when she got the call telling her the part of Karen Walker was hers. She was then pulled over for making an illegal U-turn, but of course she didn't care.

As for the role of Jack McFarland, "after Sean's audition there was just no one else for the part," says James. After impressing the room with his portrayal of Jack, Sean turned around before he left, saying "Stop looking at my ass, Mutchnick." Everyone loved it. "That was so bold and audacious," says David.

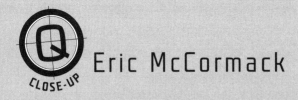

Eric McCormack

Eric McCormack was born on April 18, 1963, in Toronto, Ontario, Canada. The future Will Truman studied acting at the Banff School of Fine Arts at Toronto's Ryerson University and spent five years with the renowned Stratford Shakespearean Festival. Eric has worked steadily in film and television since 1986. Before *Will & Grace*, one of Eric's most memorable characters was Col. Clay Mosby on *Lonesome Dove: The Outlaw Years*.

Although Eric originally turned the part down, he came to love the character of Will Truman. "Will Truman has become so real for me, I actually worry about him," says McCormack on the show's Web site. "I'll go to bed thinking, 'I hope the poor bugger's getting a little action.'"

Aside from being straight and married, Eric was a natural fit for the fastidious, witty gay lawyer. Growing up, Eric's interests were in theater, not sports. "I was called a fag since I was two," McCormack said in an interview with the *New York Times* in 2000. "I'm a better leading actor as a gay man than I've ever been in a straight role . . . I'm just being me."

Eric won an Emmy Award for Outstanding Lead Actor in a Comedy series in 2001 and was nominated in 2000, 2003, and 2005. He received five Golden Globe nominations for Best Performance by an Actor in a Television Series, Musical or Comedy. At the Edinburgh International Television Festival in 2006, Eric said of his time on the set of *Will & Grace*: "The experience day-to-day was about as perfect as you can get."

After *Will & Grace*, Eric created Big Cattle Productions and produced the improvised half-hour comedy *Lovesprings International* for Lifetime Television. The show centered around the high jinks of a matchmaking service in Tarzana, California. Megan Mullally and Sean Hayes both guest-starred. McCormack recently completed production on the film *What You Wish For*, which he wrote and directed.

CHAPTER TWO

America Loves Gays, Jews, and Pill Poppers! Who Knew?

QUOTE

"You knew it was a hit on pilot night. There was an electricity in the air."

—James Burrows, Series Director

HAVING A SHOW with a gay leading man, two happy fag hags, and a vamping queen proved less problematic than all parties involved originally feared. "David Nevins, Joanne Alfano, and Warren Littlefield were all very supportive," says David of NBC's upper brass. Writer and Executive Producer Jon Kinnally has a theory as to why *Will & Grace* didn't get more flak from conservatives: "Monica Lewinsky broke. We came on the air,

SHOW NIGHT AND SHIPOOPI

"It was great. Hearing the audience laugh. I loved Tuesday nights."

—James Burrows, Series Director

"The actors were so great if you threw them a new line. The staff would huddle in a scrum and come up with line changes. The audience and the actors loved it. After the taping, the writers and actors would go back to the bungalows where we wrote and worked. Eric had done *The Music Man* on Broadway, and there was a sign commissioned that read "Shipoopi" hanging on the wall. We had a disco ball over the writer's table and a bar in the writers' room that we only used on show night."

—Tracy Poust, Writer and Executive Producer

"Gregory Hines, Matt Damon, Minnie Driver... everyone came. Eric usually closed out the bar. After Eric did *Music Man*, the post-show party came to be called 'Shipoopi.'"

—Jon Kinnally, Writer and Executive Producer

"Show night was always fun, and playful. The director, Jim Burrows, who is brilliant, ran show night expeditiously. We'd shoot each scene a couple of times. First time we shot what we'd rehearsed that week, while the writers stood around watching the scene play on a monitor, and listening to the audience reaction. Second time through, the writers would punch up some of the joke lines, or add lines to clarify the scene, and we'd perform the new rewrites on the spot."

—Tim Bagley ("Larry")

"We had beautifully catered food from Sandy from Fort Worth, who fed us for years. You had a live band. You had a DJ that would kick in with music the minute the director said 'Cut.' You had the whole audience that they plied with sugar all night to keep 'em. Eric would grab the mic and talk to the audience. Debra would talk to the audience.... When there's a hit show like that there's an electricity in the air. We would do one take as written. Period. Immediately we would take a moment with all the writers huddled and they'd come up with newer, funnier, bawdier jokes. It would get progressively dirty. We'd do one for the audience that would never get on the air to keep the audience going. One time Megan [Karen] said to Shelly [Rosario], 'Where are my slippers?' Shelly's character was supposed to say, 'Follow your drunken footsteps backwards. You'll find them.' Someone ran in and told her to say something else. Megan said again, 'Where are my slippers?' and Shelly said, 'If they were up your ass you'd know.' All hell broke loose. Show night was just a party. And I think that came through on air. The producers were smart to keep it that way."

—Leslie Jordan ("Beverly Leslie")

Q FACT

Will & Grace was taped in front of live audience on Tuesday nights at the CBS Studio Center in Studio City, California. On Wednesday mornings they would hold table reads. Table reads are when the cast reads—usually cold-reads—the script they'll be shooting in a little less than a week.

and by the time people who protest paid attention it was too late. We were a hit!"

The Writers: A Good Solid Dysfunctional Family

After the show was picked up, Max and David hired their team of writers. Among the Season 1 staff were future *Sex and the City* creator Michael Patrick King, as well as Tracy Poust and Jon Kinnally, who stayed with the show through the entire series, starting as staff writers and ending their run as executive producers and show runners. *Will & Grace* was the writing duo's first interview in television. Jon had been working as a cater waiter and Tracy was teaching spin classes when she wasn't busy starring in an Off-Broadway play she and Jon wrote about a woman who lost her vagina (played by an actress in a costume Tracy describes as "amazing!"). Michael Patrick King knew them from the New York theater world and told David and Max they had to meet them. "It's in the room with those two," he said. Tracy, a "gay man in a woman's body," according to David, and Jon, an actual gay man, had the right sensibilities for the show. Plus they were really funny.

In Season 1, the writing staff was so small that "everyone wrote. Everyone got to put something in," says Tracy. She and Jon wrote three scripts that year—not bad for their first year as television writers. Jon and Tracy's first script, Episode 7 of Season 1, "Boo! Humbug!" had to be written in one weekend. They originally wrote a different script, but as new writers they ran into problems with the script's produceability. "It was about my stuff getting sold after my apartment was broken into. Looking at my belongings on a blanket in Astor Place," says Tracy, "It became unproduceable because it all took place outside."

QUOTE

"The writers were a good solid dysfunctional family. Everyone was invested. They cared about what they did."

—Series Co-Creator David Kohan

THE TABLE READS

"When you have a hit show on the air like *Will & Grace*, those table reads can be so much pressure. There's fifty people there. A lot of them are Max and David's people, but there are also these Suits and they change every week. You think, 'Who are these people?!' Then there's the whispering. But at those readings, I noticed that the only thing that mattered between Debra and Eric and Megan and Sean was making the other one laugh. After saying a line, they didn't even look at Jimmy. If they got a laugh out of their other cast members, we moved on. That's what was important."

—Leslie Jordan ("Beverly Leslie")

"I think my favorite moment of *Will & Grace* was the Wednesday morning table reads. Eric, Debra, Sean, and Megan sat on one side of a rectangular table arrangement with a few writers next to them, as sometimes a writer had to sub for a guest star. The show runners—Gary, Tracy, Jon, and Jimmy—sat to their right; Max, Dave, and the rest of the writers sat across from them; and the guest stars—or semi-regulars, like Rosario and Beverly Leslie—sat at the other end. The rest of the seats were filled with production people, especially crew heads busy scouring the script for set, lighting, and wardrobe clues, as well as reps from NBC.

"There was still the high of Tuesday night's filming with absolutely none of the glamour! Eric was usually there first, knocking back coffee and schmoozing with everyone. Sean would come in with the same bound-less energy he had during the filming. Debra would come in with Roman, her son, before he was spirited off for a nap, and Megan invariably showed up with no signs of residual Karen. I was always blown away by how gracious the actors were: whenever we had a guest star, whether it was Britney Spears or someone with one line, each one of them would go over, introduce themselves, and make them feel welcomed. I know I'm making it sound like 'isn't it wonderful! They have manners!' but keep in mind that they just worked a twelve-hour day on their feet, at the top of their game, and with very little downtime they were back for more. They might have done press interviews in the morning or gone to wardrobe fittings or tried to say hi to their friends and family. But there was never an ego; they were always gracious hosts happy to share their 'home' for a week.

"So here they were, no makeup, yesterday's hair now collapsed from a hard night's sleep, in sweats and, for Megan especially, comfortable shoes—real people, real friends. Nine times out of ten, they'd spoken to each other on their way in to work.

"And then Jimmy Burrows would read the name of the episode and the writer's name. Every single week, the cast would boo when the writer's name was men-tioned, and every week it got a huge laugh. When Jimmy would say, 'Fade in, Will and Grace's apartment, day,' it was like when the Wizard of Oz turned to color. These tired, normal, friendly, slightly schlumpy people would turn into the icons we knew them as. They didn't just read the script; they performed it. Remember, this was the first time they knew the story and heard the jokes, and they laughed and encouraged each other and were genuinely delighted by their characters. Those readings were an unbridled joy."

—Janis Hirsch, Co-Executive Producer

The Writers' Rituals

Once the show was picked up for another season, Max and David started a tradition called Story Camp. Every June, the writers would get together and just talk. Out of these discussions evolved story lines for both character arcs and stand-alone episodes. "Seasons were most successful when we came up with an arc like 'We want Grace to meet someone, get married, and then have the marriage fall apart,'" says Tracy.

Story Camp was just one of many writer traditions. Every morning in the writers' room, the scribes would participate in Host Chat during which everyone would go around the room and say something about the night before, or recount a tawdry tale from their lives. Those morning chats inspired many episodes. "Max was the best raconteur by far," says David. "Max can take any little situation and make it really entertaining. He understood the camp value of a bad date."

Another morning ritual involved physical activity. "We would close the door because it was so embarrassing," says Tracy. "There were hoots and clicks and finger snapping that Max made us do. It was a whole choreographed routine." After Eric McCormack starred in *The Music Man* on Broadway, the writers would end their routine by saying, "Shipoopi," which was a number from the musical. "That show was a lot of fun," remembers Tracy.

Out of the Closet and into the Frying Pan

Luckily, most of the letters *Will & Grace* received were positive. "We got letters from kids saying they didn't feel so alone," says Tracy. "You felt like you were doing something that was making a difference." However, there was one letter that sparked a lot of controversy: a request from Mike Haley, a Public Policy/Youth & Gender Specialist with the Evangelical group Focus on the Family, to meet with Jon Kinnally about Episode 22 of Season 2, "Girls, Interrupted." "Focus on the Family complaining was a big deal," recalls Jon.

Jon, an openly gay man, had been one of the writers on the episode about an "ex-gay ministry" that Jack infiltrates and eventually disrupts by leading everyone back out of the closet. "They could not have been more polite," says David of Focus on the Family's letter. They felt the show denigrated people who had overcome 'something painful' in their lives." Naturally, the staff couldn't resist writing a response to the letter. "We felt that the whole idea of turning someone straight was idiotic," says Jon. "The writers spent an hour in the room composing the most offensive letter they could think of. The gist was: "We know where you're going with this . . . you're hitting on me . . ." says David. "Nobody said we should try to break stories. Everyone contributed

A WAR OF WORDS

Dear Mr. Kinnally,

I am writing to request a meeting with you regarding a recent episode of *Will and Grace*. The show in question grossly misrepresented thousands of individuals struggling to come out of homosexuality. As a former gay man, and now a national spokesman and expert on homosexuality and youth issues for Focus on the Family—one of the country's largest organizations who, among other things, assists gays and lesbians who desire to be heterosexual—I know first-hand how frustrating and painful it is to be mocked by those who haven't taken the time to find out what this process is all about. I'm specifically talking about references in the show to former homosexuals, and those wrestling with their sexual identity, as "freaks," "self-loathing closet cases," "morally wrong" and as members of "cults." Nowhere in this episode are we portrayed as honest men and women seeking help.

You may vehemently disagree with this position, but I'd at least like the opportunity to sit down with you and talk about it. Our conversation may not change your mind about the possibility of coming out of homosexuality, but at the very least it will put a real face behind the caricature you depicted on prime time TV. And in the end, hopefully it will encourage you to think twice before ridiculing the belief systems of those who differ from you. With that in mind, please respectfully consider my request, Mr. Kinnally. Thank you.

Sincerely,
Mike Haley
Public Policy/Youth Gender Specialist
Focus on the Family

Dear Mr. Haley,

I received your letter dated June 9, and was very interested in your point of view. The issues you raised are the very same ones that we on the *Will & Grace* writing staff debate on a daily basis. Our decision to present the story on the ex-gay ministry was solely in the interest of creating the most comedic episode possible. And it was certainly not our intention to offend you in any way. But come on, Mike, even you've got to admit that fags trying to pretend they're straight is pretty darn funny.

In response to your request for a meeting, well, I think I can read between the lines on that one. I'm about 6'1", brown hair, green eyes and I'm into rollerblading, baking cookies, and cleaning up afterwards. My dislikes include game-playing, negative attitudes, and condoms.

If any of this interests you, I can be found every Sunday at the Brunch and Beer Bust at the Motherlode in West Hollywood. I do hope you show, because I like you, I am an expert on homosexuality, and in my expert opinion, "this hard-to-get thing" you're playing is Hot, Hot, Hot!

Respectfully,
Jon Kinnally
Executive Story Editor
Will & Grace

P.S. Keep on watchin'

and spent a joyous hour composing this thing." Max originally wanted to put his name on the letter, but was talked out of it lest he get in serious trouble with the upper brass. Jon Kinnally volunteered to be the letter's official author. "He has a good counterculture streak going through him," says David.

Focus on the Family was outraged by the writers' response. They sent a copy of the writers' letter to the head of NBC and to V.I.P.s at GE, NBC's parent company. "It was just a goof," says David, "indicative of the kind of group we were."

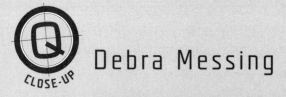

Debra Messing

Debra Messing was born on August 15, 1968, in Brooklyn, New York, but was raised in rural East Greenwich, Rhode Island, near Providence. In 1986, she was Rhode Island's Junior Miss. Like Grace, Debra is proud of her Jewish ancestry, though she considers herself more culturally Jewish than religious. Debra majored in theater arts at Brandeis University before entering New York University's premier Graduate Acting Program. While there, she met her husband, actor/writer Daniel Zelman. In New York, Debra worked in theater where she received praise for her performance in a pre-Broadway workshop production of Tony Kushner's *Angels in America*. A small role on *NYPD Blue* soon followed. Debra worked steadily in television and film, including *A Walk in the Clouds* with Keanu Reeves. In 1995, she entered the realm of leading lady, starring in the Fox sitcom *Ned and Stacy* for two seasons.

Debra was working on an ABC drama, *Prey*, when her agents approached her about Grace Adler. The smart writing and novel premise intrigued the actress. "I come from the New York theater world, and I have a lot of gay male friends, so this friendship of Will and Grace's isn't such a stretch," Debra told *Complete Woman* magazine in 1999.

As Grace, Debra was able to exercise the full range of her comic talents, from pratfalls to Jewish neurosis. Playing a klutzy character allowed Debra to show off her physical comedy chops. In Season 6, when Debra was pregnant with her son, Roman, both she and the writers had to explore other avenues for Grace's jokes. In an interview with *American Jewish Life* magazine, she said, "It was depressing, but fascinating because it was a test for the writers and for me. They had to make me funny in a more verbal way. It was tricky and when it worked it was incredibly satisfying."

Her performance earned Debra six Emmy nominations for Outstanding Lead Actress in a Comedy Series, and in 2003 she took home the award. She also garnered six Golden Globe nominations for Best Actress in a Television or Comedy and won the 2001 TV Guide Award for Best Actress of the Year in a Comedy Series.

In 2002, a dream of Debra's came true when she was cast as Woody Allen's girlfriend in his film *Hollywood Ending*. Woody Allen described Debra to Jeannie Williams for *USA Today* as a "natural comic talent . . . beautiful, very, very gifted. She lights up everything she does."

Since *Will & Grace*, Debra was again nominated for an Emmy and Golden Globe for her performance as jilted wife Molly Kagan in the USA mini-series *The Starter Wife*. The program was so popular, it was picked up as a regular series, which will star Debra.

The Fab Four and the Woman Who Cleaned Up After Them

QUOTE

"The characters were unlike anything else on the air. The jokes were so funny, you forgot that Will and Jack were gay, Karen took pills, and Grace was a neurotic Jew. You started laughing at them and then you realized what it meant for the community to have a gay leading man and a Jewish leading woman."

—Series Director, James Burrows

Will Truman, played by Eric McCormack

QUOTE

"I'm 5'11", I'm not into games, I like horseback riding, skiing, and men who aren't afraid to cry."

—Will Truman

Will Truman Esq. was television's first leading gay man, and as of this writing, two years after *Will & Grace* went off the air, he remains television's only gay leading man. By default, that makes Grace television's most prominent gay wife, the first lady of fag haggery. The two friends share some serious homojo (homo mojo): They finish each other's sentences and always know what the other is thinking. The perfect display of their mind meld are those fierce rounds of Pyramid where, with just one word, they know each other's answers. A classic example: Will: "Bangs." Grace: "Nancy McKeon."

Fastidious as Grace is flighty, Wilma, as Karen calls

him, has a few surprising quirks, considering his polished and reserved nature. For instance, despite living in an apartment where the doors are never locked and characters are bound to burst in at any moment, Will is partial to reading on his couch, buck naked. Nathan (Woody Harrelson), Grace's boyfriend in Seasons 3 and 4, once caught Will in the act and warned him, "That's a nasty paper cut waiting to happen." Years later, Leo, Grace's husband, walked in on Will reading and startled him so much that Will hurt his favorite "bookmark."

Ain't No Closet Big Enough

"You're gay, Will! OK? You're gayer than the day is long. You're Marvin Gaye. And let me tell you somethin'—ain't no closet big enough."

—Jack McFarland to Will Truman in 1985

Born to WASP parents Marilyn (Blythe Danner) and George (Sydney Pollack) in Connecticut, Will wasn't raised in an outwardly homophobic environment, but his mother would purposely sabotage his musical numbers at family Christmas parties. During his sophomore year of high school, Will had an epiphany while playing basketball: "Jay Barr and I went up for a rebound. Our stomachs touched, and, by the time I came down, I was gay." Claire (Megyn Price), Will's high school girlfriend, wasn't privy to this information, though her suspicions may have been raised when, to avoid making out with her after the prom, Will crashed their car.

In 1985, Will was dating Grace, who lived across the hall in their dorm at Columbia University. Grace was perfect in every way except she had lady parts. At some point that year a guy we never meet named Max Stokes threw a party that both Will and Jack attended. At that party, Jack, who was still in high school, told Will he was gay. Will ignored Jack's opinion and was saddened to run into him a little while later at a party in Will's dorm in the 9th episode of Season 3, "Lows in the Mid-Eighties." Again Jack insists that Will is gay. Will denies it and Jack says, "Well, this well-worn copy of the *Dreamgirls* soundtrack begs to differ." Before Will kicks him out, Jack gives him his card. Later, when Grace brings Will to her home in Schenectady for a Thanksgiving break of love, Will panics and calls Jack from the bathroom to tell him he's *really* not gay. Jack, of course, calls him on his denial and sets him (un)straight.

Will, unable to face the truth, climbs back into bed with Grace only to panic again and propose marriage as a way of putting off the big boink. Minutes later, Will realizes he can't continue with the charade and outs himself to Grace. Grace, heartbroken and angry, doesn't speak to Will for a year, although Will tries to contact her repeatedly. Right after they split, Will takes one last, drunken stab at heterosexuality with a girl named

Diane (later played by Mira Sorvino). The sex, awful for him, sadly turns out to be the best of Diane's life. Over the Grace-less year, Jack guides Will through the process of dating men, and even helps Will break the ice with one guy at a club by secretly bribing him. Later, Will writes a play in college about his coming-out experience, titled *Bye-bisexual*.

Will and Grace reconnect and soon become best friends again. During the nineties Will dates Michael for seven years. After he breaks up with Michael and Grace breaks up with her fiancé, Danny, they become roommates in Will's Upper West Side pad.

Will's Infamously Un-infamous Love Life

For a handsome, witty, intelligent lawyer with a great Upper West Side apartment, Will suffered a serious man drought for most of the show. To some, Will's nearly sexless existence, especially in the earlier years, lacked realism. Leslie Jordan, an openly gay actor who played the poodle-sized, fey, Southern closet case Beverly Leslie, heard complaints about Will's love life in the gay community. "They would ask me, 'Why does Will never have a boyfriend?' and 'Why isn't there kissing?'" says Leslie. "Max and David were smart. They knew what their parameters were at the time. It had to be digestible to Middle America but still have a wonderful message. America welcomed these characters into their homes and laughed and loved and learned," he adds.

As the show gained popularity and Emmys, the writers felt America really saw Will as a person, not just a symbol of gay culture. As they would for any other adored TV character, people were rooting for him to find love. "We thought, 'we're a hit!' We can approach the network to do a gayer Will episode," says writer Jon Kinnally. While Will's trysts grew in number, he didn't have a long-term boyfriend until Season 6, when Italian cop Vince (Bobby Cannavale) came along. But Will's bad luck in relationships was more a function of his being a sitcom character than a gay man. Will, and Grace too for that matter, weren't supposed to be lucky in love, because watching well-adjusted people take part in healthy relationships is as funny as cat food.

"Gay or straight, the only person who's had a long-term relationship on the show is Karen, and we've never met Stan and that's what's kept that alive. To add someone to the show for me or for [Grace] is a very big decision," says Eric in his commentary for the Season 1 DVD. "It wasn't 'we don't want to have a gay lover.' It was 'we don't want a lover, period.'" Finding the right man to play Will's boyfriend also proved challenging. Max told *The Advocate*, "It's really hard to find an actor who can hold his own with Eric McCormack and play a gay character with the integrity he plays it with. . . . There [are] a lot of men on the cutting-room floor." Plus Will was not without his faults. He could be controlling and preoccupied by what others thought of him. But as the series drew to a close, Will got the ending many were hoping he would: he found long-lasting love (and a family) with Vince.

Grace Adler, played by Debra Messing

Bottle-redhead Jewess Grace Elizabeth Adler is a talented interior designer, a quick wit, a shockingly terrible singer, and more likely to leave the seat up than her best friend, Will Truman. Grace's uncouth qualities are a perfect foil for Will's controlling, fussy ways. "Grace is very dedicated and disciplined when it comes to her professional life but her personal life isn't nearly so together, and Will is her stabilizing force," says Debra Messing on the NBC Web site. "She's a little neurotic, and she knows Will is the only person who understands her and can help her put things in perspective. But Grace is also a lot of fun, and her humor helps balance Will's more serious personality. They're the kind of best friends who know each other's history and can finish each other's sentences."

Grace is confident in her skills as a designer and even a seductress, often placing herself in the pantheon of red-haired beauties like Julia Roberts circa *Pretty Woman* and Rita Hayworth. Although Grace is undeniably pretty, her flaws—large feet, klutzy moves, flat chest, propensity to overeat, and deafening vocal range—often provide great fodder for laughs not just from Will, Karen, and Jack but from Grace herself.

Debra was also a fan of Grace's flaws and tone-deaf crooning, telling *American Jewish Life* magazine in 2006, "To me, the bad singing, no pun intended, takes the grace off her . . . I didn't want to be the pretty straight woman. I knew I wouldn't be happy. I grew up watching Lucille Ball and Carol Burnett with curtain rods in her arms, falling down stairs. To me, that's funny."

Grace is proud of her Jewish heritage and joyfully mentions family members with hard-on-the-throat Yiddish-influenced names like "Uncle Hachel." And she can't help herself from blurting, "Oy, goyim," when she's forced to bear witness to the WASPy antics of Will's inexpressive family.

When she was cast as Grace, Debra, also a proud member of the tribe, was thrilled. In her initial audition for *Ned and Stacy* (a Fox sitcom she starred in before *Will & Grace*), Debra was told she was too "wholesome." She told *The Jewish Journal* in 2003, "They wanted a neurotic Jew from New York, and I said, hello, I'm right here!" Grace gave Debra a chance to finally bring her neurotic Jewish personality to the small screen: "I thought it would be great if Grace were open and unapologetic about being Jewish; if her Jewishness were just a fact, the way it's a fact that Will is gay."

From Schenectady to the Queens

QUOTE

"I'm a good girl from Schenectady. I went to Sunday school for ten years. I was sixteen before I let Bobby Kay go to second!"

—Grace Adler

Grace began her life in Schenectady, New York, as the middle child to wannabe stage legend Bobbi Adler (Debbie Reynolds) and the *Kojak*-loving, crabby Martin (Alan Arkin). She later attended Columbia University in Manhattan, where she met Will. It was love at first sight for both of them, only Will's love was platonic while Grace's was decidedly lustier. In Season 3's flashback extravaganza episode, "Lows in the Mid-Eighties," Grace brings Will home to Schenectady for Thanksgiving and relationship consummation. Will does whatever he can think of to delay their sexual milestone, even going so far as proposing marriage. Grace is thrilled. Sadly, their engagement is short-lived, as moments later Will comes out to Grace and her family. The two don't talk for a year but after a chance encounter at a D'Agostino's, they renew their friendship and embark on becoming best friends, sometime roommates, and many years later in-laws (when their children marry).

At the start of the series, Grace is engaged to Danny, an insensitive boyfriend who high-fives her after sex. Grace leaves Danny at the altar and moves in with Will for the rest of the season. Season 2 finds Grace living across the hall and dating up a storm, which Will observes as making up for her "headgear years."

Over the years Grace dates a variety of men, including Will's smooth-talking boss Ben Doucette (Gregory Hines), unkempt neighbor Nathan (Woody Harrelson), greeting-card writer Nick (Ed Burns), married high-school sweetheart Tom (Eric Stoltz), among (many) others. After a whirlwind romance, Grace marries Dr. Marvin "Leo" Markus, a Southern-born,

Jewish doctor and the only boyfriend of Grace's who never complains about her close relationship with Will. Their marriage hits the skids rather quickly as Leo's work with Doctors Without Borders takes him all over the world and, for one night in Cambodia, into another woman's bed. Grace and Leo get divorced but eventually reunite and raise their daughter, Lila, together.

Karen (Delaney St. Croix Popeil Finster) Walker, played by Megan Mullally

Karen Walker, the saucy, bisexual socialite, is Grace's inept assistant and trophy wife of Stan Walker for most of the series. Although she is a gazzillionaire, Karen chooses to work for Grace to keep herself "down to earth," which in Karenspeak means loaded up on booze, drugs, and delivering tactless, razor-sharp assessments to people in a high-pitched squeak. She often demands explanations from Grace about her wardrobe choices. Casting a judgmental glare over Grace's outfit du jour, Karen will ask, "Honey, what's this? What's happening? What's going on here?"

In addition to being Will and Grace's go-to for verbal abuse, Karen also functions as one half of the other couple on *Will & Grace*. That couple, of course, is Jack and Karen. Karen, with her wigs, designer taste, and high camp value is the natural complement to diva Jack McFarland. Their characters seem like they were crafted to make trouble together, but the relationship between Jack and Karen came as a surprise even to the show's creators. Max says on the commentary to the Season 1 DVD, "We had no idea about the Karen and Jackness of it all. It was a show about Will and Grace. It was a bonus to realize there's another couple on that stage. It's fabulous."

The Eureka moment happened in the second episode of Season 1, "A New Lease on Life," when Karen and Jack first meet. After taking in an eyeful of the coiffed hottie with the killer rack, Jack declares: "Well, Peter, Paul and Mary, you are fabulous!" Soon after, Jack asks Karen to touch stomachs and she's all for it. "We wrote this scene where he's intrigued by her and she plays coy and he asks her to touch stomachs," says David. "She says, 'You're a freak for asking me that,' and then goes along with it. It felt like 'I get you. You're kind of a weird kindred spirit of mine.'"

Like their on-screen counterparts, Sean Hayes and Megan Mullally love to maul each other. Eric McCormack says Megan and Sean "have groped in a way that's not even prime time." In PlanetOut.com's celebrity profile of Megan, she's quoted as saying, "If [Sean] walked in right now, he'd grab my boob and start dry-humping me. . . . If we were presented to the queen of England, I'd probably be grabbing his package."

Aside from gropage and dry humping, Karen and Jackie enjoy a close friendship, letting their larger-than-life personalities land them in all kinds of adventures.

Karen has a much more distant relationship with her staff, often referring to them by their job title instead of their names: Driver, Pastry Chef, Chef, Pharmacist, Back-up Pharmacist, etc. One exception is Rosario, her maid since around 1985. Rosario can dish out abusive zingers just as well as Karen, but they do genuinely care for each other. When RoRo is nearly deported, Karen makes Jack marry her for a green card.

From Fags to Riches and Back Again: The Karen Walker Story

Karen Walker is all rich lady suits and Botox, but Karen Delaney was born of modest means to a con-artist mother named Lois (Suzanne Pleshette). Young Karen was often a pawn in her mother's various schemes. When Lois ran a scam on a he/she Karen dated, the future Mrs. Walker had enough. Although Karen grew up poor, she seems to have repressed a lot of the details of life below the millionaire line. When the gang takes her to a Laundromat, she's very confused.

Karen ran away from Lois and married a man with the last name of St. Croix, and then later married another man who went by Popeil. Nothing is ever said about either of Karen's previous marriages, but by 1985 she was single and turning down overtures of love from a man named Clayton, the Sultan of Bahran (Habibi Shoshani Padush Al-Kabir), and Martina Navratilova because she was in love with a 900-pound, hairy married man named Stanley Walker. At some point she also had an affair with Ronald Reagan and was the face of "Atooshi Kodki!" a Japanese energy drink made of vitamins and nicotine.

Karen and Stan finally tie the knot in 1995, and Karen becomes a fairly bad stepmother to Stanley's son, Mason, known to Karen as "the fat one," and daughter,

QUOTE

JACK: "Karen. It is a Laundromat. People come here to clean their clothes, then they reuse them."
KAREN: "Why, poor people are just plain clever. I wonder, why they can't figure out a way to make more money?"

Olivia, aka "the girl." Karen is faithful to Stan for years, but when he gets sent to prison for tax evasion, Karen has a brief affair with the smooth-talking Lionel Banks (Rip Torn) and they do "everything but."

During his incarceration, Stan hooks up with a fetching cockney cafeteria wench named Lorraine Finster (Minnie Driver). Stan and Lorraine continue their affair throughout Season 5, much to Karen's dismay. At the end of the season, Stan unexpectedly croaks while on top of Lorraine. Stan leaves his vast fortune to Karen, and later Lorraine throws Karen overboard at Stan's memorial at sea. In Season 6, Karen tries to find Lorraine but instead meets her father, Lyle Finster

(John Cleese). Lyle is as classy as Lorraine is unrefined. Karen falls for him. The two are quickly married in Vegas, where Jennifer Lopez performs at the wedding reception. However, Lyle proves too controlling, and Karen dumps him after the wedding toast. Karen dates here and there, but never truly gets over her dearly departed Stanley.

When Karen finds out at the beginning of Season 8 that Stan faked his death to avoid trouble with the mob, she is unable to forgive him. Karen has a fling with Malcolm Widmark (Alec Baldwin), the shadowy government agent who assisted Stanley with his subterfuge, but once Karen learns Stanley gave Malcolm his permission to date the ex-Mrs. Walker, Karen runs back to Stan. Their reunion is short-lived and the two get divorced in the series finale.

Karen supports Jack financially for most of the series, not from her income as Grace's lazy assistant, but from Walker money. After their divorce, Stanley's fortune is deemed a fraud, and Karen's settlement is rendered worthless. Karen pushes Jack to enter into a "business relationship" with her rival, the pint-size queen Beverly Leslie (Leslie Jordan), so that he can support her the way she's always supported him. Ultimately, Karen can't let Jack go through with the sexual depravity of bedding Leslie, but before Jack dumps him, Leslie is blown away while standing on a balcony. Jack inherits his fortune after all and becomes Karen's benefactor.

Q FACT

Karen's alias in bars, taco joints, and bowling allies is Anastasia Beaverhousen.

SOME REAL-LIFE INSPIRATION

ROSARIO: Rosario was the name of Series Co-Creator Max Mutchnick's housekeeper. She would answer the door wearing a "My lawyer is a shark" T-shirt. As of 2008, she cleans Sean Hayes's house.

JACK: "There were a few people that were the inspiration for Jack," says Series Co-Creator David Kohan. One man, Jack Deamer, a friend of Max's, believed he was the sole inspiration for Jack and even sued Max.

KAREN: During college, Max was amazed by the wealth of his friend, Karen, says David. "At one point he was helicoptered from Boston to New York" by her family. After college, Karen announced she was going to work as an assistant because she wanted to "stay in touch with the regular people, be a part of the great unwashed," says David. He adds, "The real Karen's personality bears no resemblance to Karen Walker's."

Jack McFarland, played by Sean Hayes

QUOTE

"Jack, blind and deaf people know you're gay. Dead people know you're gay."

—Will

Jack McFarland is the jazz-handsy, over-the-top queen to Will's reserved, GQ Gay. Jack can veer into stereo-typical gay man territory with his campy fluttering, but part of Jack's charm is his overwhelming comfort with his identity—he doesn't care if he acts stereotypically. Jack is going to be "Just Jack," and if people don't like it, it's *just* their loss.

Jack's passions include himself, his good looks, men, acting, dancing, *Buffy the Vampire Slayer,* his parrot Guapo, his dog Klaus Von Puppy, his recipe for "Garlic Jazz," musicals, gay icons like Cher, and his hag, Karen. Jack and Karen, unlike Will and Grace, rarely fight. Jack is somewhat of a kept man in that Karen funds his life-style, but theirs is a symbiotic relationship as Karen finds Jackie endlessly amusing. Off camera, Sean and Megan Mullally's relationship is equally boisterous. Megan says, "Sean and I crack each other up in a way that borders on mental illness." Jack and Karen love to make fun of Will and Grace's co-dependence. As Karen tells Jack in Season 7's "Kiss and Tell," "If we do everything together, then what are we? Will and Grace." They never want to be those two.

Jack's various interests have led him to pursue a vast array of careers, including actor, massage therapist, cabaret performer, playwright, "salesgirl" at Banana Republic and Barneys New York, Kevin Bacon's assistant, magician, acting teacher, backup dancer to Jennifer Lopez (and almost Janet Jackson), student nurse, television executive, talk-show host, and finally TV's Detective Chuck Rafferty on *The Badge*. He also runs Jacques, a one-table café in the hallway outside his apartment. Karen is a frequent customer.

"Will's door was always unlocked so Jack could enter with a flourish. When Jack came in you knew something funny was going to happen."

—James Burrows, Series Director

Jack McFarland Since 1969

Jack was born in 1969 to Judith McFarland (Veronica Cartwright) and her husband Daniel (Beau Bridges). Growing up, Jack believed Daniel was his father, but in Season 2 Jack learns that his biological father was actually a man in a Nixon mask who knocked boots with Judith in a pool at a key party. While Jack and his father had never been close on account of Jack's disinterest in typically hetero activities like sports and girls, Jack is still devastated by the news. He goes on a quest to find his real father, Joe Black, only to discover that "the loins of his fruit" died several years earlier. Jack receives the sad news about his father on the same day Jack's biological son, Elliot, tracks him down. When Jack was seventeen he needed money for a jacket, so he donated sperm to the New York Family Clinic, where a gay nurse, Bonnie (Rosie O'Donnell), used the sample of the "ballet dancer and model who enjoys long walks on the beach" on herself. After an initial period of adjustment, Jack and Elliot enjoy a close relationship that reveals Jack's less egocentric qualities.

A key moment in Jack's life occurred in 1985 when he met Will at Matt Stoke's party and told Will he was gay. A little while later, at a party in Will's dorm, Will runs into Jack rifling through his closet. When Will catches Jack, he asks him, "What are you doing in the closet?" Jack responds, "I could ask the same of you." Later, Will, hiding in a bathroom to avoid sex with Grace, calls Jack, panicking. Jack coaches Will through his coming out, and in the process falls in love. When Jack expresses his feelings, Will explains that while

Jack has been his sherpa though the "Himalayas of . . . of him-a-laying," he doesn't see him as a love interest. Voice breaking, Jack plays his confession off as a final "test" of Will's success as a gay man. For the rest of their friendship, Jack refers to the lithe Will with his full head of hair as bald and fat. Sour grapes? Maybe . . .

Even though Jack was instrumental in Will's coming out, Jack didn't reveal his choice in dance partners to his mother until Season 2's "Homo for the Holidays." After he delivers the big news, Karen helpfully reminds Judith that "when you're old and in diapers, a gay son will know how to keep you away from chiffon and backlighting."

Jack's mother is completely accepting of her son's homosexuality and admits there may have been a few clues when he was growing up that he might swing that way, like his preference for the nursery rhyme "Rub-a-dub-dub, three men in a tub."

At the end of the first season, Jack marries Karen's maid, Rosario, so that she can stay in the country. Of the marriage he says, "Oh, my very own sexless marriage, just like Will and Grace."

Jack isn't one for long-term relationships and has countless trysts throughout the series. His only serious boyfriend is Stuart Lamarack (Dave Foley), whom he dates for several months in Season 6. Stuart and Jack are so serious that they nearly move in together, but their relationship falls apart when Jack cheats. Jack's final relationship of the series is another arranged union by Karen. In "The Finale," Beverly Leslie, the rich, closeted mini-queen, wants Jack to be his new

JACK'S THEATER OF LIFE

Jack and the Beanstalk
17-year-old Jack's one-man show.

Just Jack (later revived as *Just Jack 2000* and *Just Jack 2001*)
Jack's legendary (in his mind) one-man cabaret act.

Love Among the Coconuts: A Caribbean Fantasy
Jack's first play after taking an inspiring class at the Learning Annex. Karen declared it a stinker and it was never performed.

Untitled Jack McFarland Fall Project Entitled Jack: A Meditation in Three Parts
Jack's second play portrays Will and Grace as terrible friends who neglected poor Jack before his untimely death. They realize the error of their ways and kill themselves to join Jack in Heaven, but when they reach

"business associate," which translates to concubine. Karen, now broke, insists Jack go through with it so that he can support her the way she has supported him over the years. Jack reluctantly agrees, but Karen stops Jack before he and Beverly do any serious business.

the pearly gates, they're told they belong "downstairs" by Karen's bawdy version of St. Peter.

"The McFarland Method"
An acting technique Jack invents when he takes over the class of his longtime acting teacher and human nightmare, Zandra. The main tenets concern hot men baring their chests, speaking in a high-pitched voice, and having great hair.

Jack Talk
Jack's talk show on gay network, Out TV. When the network changes owners and becomes a platform for patriotic propaganda, Jack is the one who's out.

The Badge
Jack plays Chuck Rafferty, a straight, alcoholic, womanizing cop on this dramatic crime series. Jack originally auditioned for Squealing Queen #3 but was so depressed, he was unable to tap into any of his acting instincts. As a result, his reserved performance lands him a huge role.

Luckily for Jack, Beverly had already made him the sole heir to his vast fortune and, when a strong wind blows Beverly off his penthouse balcony, Jack becomes a millionaire. Karen and Jack live together for at least twenty years after the series ends.

Q FACT:
Just . . . Too Much

Whenever Jack mentions the title of his cabaret act, he frames his face with his hands, a gesture he modified over the years under the names *Jack 2000* and later *Jack 2001*. The *Just Jack* hand moves were popular with fans but all the vogue-ing got out of control. Megan Mullally told *Entertainment Weekly*, "Sean went through a period where everybody he met was saying, 'Just Jack!' and holding their hands around their face. That gets a little old."

Rosario Inez Consuelo Yolanda Salazar, played by Shelley Morrison

Rosario, Karen's acerbic, put-upon maid, enjoys a love/hate relationship with her employer. Their verbal sparring often escalates to threats of death or deportation.

Rosario has a style all her own: light blue maid's uniform, white apron, knee highs, orthopedic shoes, dark glasses, and occasionally a Members Only jacket. In addition to her signature look, Rosario also has a distinctive voice—deep, guttural, at times sympathetic, other times dripping with bitterness. Shelley Morrison credits her mother for inspiring Rosario's low voice. In an interview with *Back Stage West* in 2004, Morrison said her mother "wouldn't suffer a fool and wouldn't take any BS. Her voice would get sixteen octaves lower when she was trying to get across a point."

CLASSIC KAREN AND ROSARIO

ROSARIO: "Yoko Ono gave me two dollars for orange Tic-Tacs—I think she likes me."
KAREN: "Oh, honey, she definitely likes you. Yeah, I just passed her in the hallway and she asked me if she could buy the big wooden statue of Sitting Bull that's in my bathroom."

ROSARIO: "This year I'm making your figgy pudding with Ajax and rat poison."

KAREN: "If it weren't for me, you'd be flying back to Cucaracha on Air Guacamole with live chickens running up and down the aisles!"

ROSARIO: "Listen, Lady, I'm gonna snap you like a twig and throw you in a bush."

The Road to Becoming RoRo

Rosario lived a very colorful life before she committed to a career of washing Karen's bras and suffering her booze-addled demands. Born in El Salvador, Rosario was a schoolteacher prior to coming to America sometime before 1985. Rosario (also called Rosie and RoRo by Karen) was a very accomplished woman with a degree in Clinical Psychology from the University of

Texas. She even danced with Jennifer Lopez in the Bronx. The two studied tap together and performed "Tea for Two" at the Shalom Retirement Center. At one point, Rosario was also in the American Ballet Theater. In Season 8, when Karen fires Rosario for lying about Stan's fake death, Rosario considers returning to the ballet. According to Jack she had already begun preparations to get her dancer's figure back by starting a "binge-purge cycle."

In 1985, Rosario was enrolled in business school and working as a cigarette girl at a trendy club. One night, Karen laments to the bartender that her new love, Stan, is married. Rosario, calling Karen "Boozo the clown," chides Karen for bringing everyone down. The two women exchange barbs and Rosario even throws in a "Listen, Lady . . ." which will become a phrase she says often in her future toiling away in Karen's manse. After a quick round of rapid-fire insults, Karen says, " I like you. Why don't you come work for me?" Rosario says "Okay" and seals her fate as Karen's servant.

In Season 1, Karen often mentions Rosario, usually in the context of a demeaning and potentially dangerous task, but she does not appear until the Season 1 finale, "Object of My Rejection." Rosario is facing deportation, so Karen gets her favorite maid hitched to Jack in a green card wedding. Originally Rosario was only supposed to appear in that one episode, but her character proved so popular that the writers brought her back in Season 2 and made her a regular in Season 3. Morrison's portrayal of the downtrodden housekeeper was too good to pass up.

While theirs is certainly not a romantic relationship,

Jack and Rosario are fond of each other. Jack even once encouraged Karen to be nicer to her maid, only to find out Rosario preferred the bickering and abuse. Rosario once strayed from Karen, working secretly for Karen's nemesis, Beverly Leslie, but Karen caught on quickly when she noticed Rosie's new Members Only jacket.

Despite their arguments, Rosario and Karen do care for each other, and Rosario stays with Karen in the twenty or so years following Will and Grace's initial estrangement. Rosario's last words to Karen on the series are: "Suck it, bitch!"

Megan Mullally

Megan Mullally was born on November 12, 1958, in Los Angeles, California, and raised in Oklahoma. Despite being far from Hollywood, show business was in her blood: her mother was a model and her father was a retired contract player for Paramount. Throughout her teens, Megan studied ballet and spent two summers at the School of American Ballet in New York City. Her commitment to dance left little time for dating. In an interview with *InStyle* magazine she said, "I never had time to have a proper boyfriend, so I spent a lot of my twenties and thirties trying to make up for it."

Mullally attended Northwestern University, where she studied English. While at Northwestern, she briefly dated actor William H. Macy. Megan worked in the Chicago theater circuit before moving to Los Angeles in 1981. Her television series debut was on *The Ellen Burstyn Show* starring Elaine Stritch and Ellen Burstyn. Before *Will & Grace*, Megan guest-starred on many sitcoms, including *Seinfeld, Frasier, Wings,* and *Ned and Stacy*, which starred Debra Messing (though they did not share a scene).

Megan was never worried about *Will & Grace* being a controversial show. Concerning the "gay thing," she said on her commentary for the Season 1 DVD, "I never thought it would cause a 'splash' because I don't consider it odd to be gay or lesbian or bi." In an interview with *The Advocate* in 1999, Megan revealed that, like

Karen, she's also bisexual: "I consider myself bisexual, and my philosophy is, everyone innately is."

For her portrayal of Karen Walker, Megan won two Emmy Awards for Outstanding Supporting Actress in a Comedy Series. In 2004, she was awarded the Golden Gate Award by the Gay & Lesbian Alliance Against Defamation (GLAAD). Upon receiving the award she said: "It doesn't matter who you love, it's that you love. Who cares if men marry men or women marry women? In San Francisco you don't care, and I applaud that. And I applaud Mayor Newsom for being so brave."

Megan enjoyed playing Karen, and not just for the awards and accolades. There was also the humping! As she told AfterElton.com, "I loved playing Karen, and I loved goofing around and humping Sean Hayes all day." In her commentary on the final episode, Debora Messing said, "I think we've all held [Megan's] breasts gently and lovingly, kind of like a puppy."

Series co-creator David Kohan thinks Karen is so appealing to the gay community because she's "someone who is so blithely content with her life and makes no apologies." Plus Karen's just fabulous.

After *Will & Grace* ended, Megan was the host of a daytime talk-variety show, *The Megan Mullally Show*, produced by NBC Universal. After the show was canceled in January 2007, Megan appeared on the comedy *Campus Ladies*, produced by co-star Eric McCormack, and the drama *Boston Legal*. More recently Megan lent her voice to the animated *Bee Movie*. She also returned to Broadway to perform in Mel Brooks's musical *Young Frankenstein*. Like her co-star Sean Hayes, Megan is a talented musician. She sings and performs with her band The Supreme Music Program. Their third album, "Free Again!" was released online in 2007 and is available at www.supremeprogram.com.

CHAPTER FOUR

The Love Interests

The Boyfriends of Will Truman

Michael, played by Chris Potter

Will spends Season 1 struggling to move on from his relationship with ex-flame Michael, who dated Will for seven years. By Season 2, Will seems to be on the road to recovery until Michael reappears in "Hey La, Hey La, My Ex-Boyfriend's Back." In the episode, Will thinks Michael hires Grace to redecorate his new townhouse to get back in Will's life. When Will confronts Michael about his desire to reunite, he ends up humiliating himself in front of Michael's new boyfriend. But it's not all doom and gloom. Ultimately the incident is just what Will needs to eventually move on to the likes of Patrick Dempsey, Taye Diggs, and Bobby Cannavale.

Matthew, played by Patrick Dempsey

Will first meets sportswriter Matthew in a Banana Republic in Season 3's "Love Plus One." Jack, who works at the store, spots the future McDreamy and declares him his. However, after minimal conversation, Jack realizes Matt is a smarty and to win his heart he'll need to use Will in a Cyrano de Bergerac scheme using Jack's sales headset and Will's words. Matthew eventually catches on, finds Will hiding in the dressing room, and gives Will his card. Will takes two months to call Matthew, fearing he'll be turned off by Will's disinterest in sports. When Will and Matthew do go out, Will pretends to be a sports nut, but the truth is revealed when a four-year-old kicks Will's butt in a basketball game. Matthew tells Will he accepts him as he is, but Will soon learns that Matthew has trouble accepting himself. Matthew introduces Will as his "brother" to his co-workers at the news station. Ultimately, Will decides he can't date someone who isn't out.

Barry, played by Dan Futterman

Barry was first introduced in Episode 513, "Fagmalion Part One: Gay It Forward," and had a four-episode "Fagmalian" arc modeled on Pygmalion.

When they first meet, Will is unimpressed with Karen's bushy-bearded cousin, the schlubby and recently out-of-the-closet Barry. But, of course, Barry is smitten with Will. Ultimately, Jack convinces Will that as "Senior Gays," they must adhere to the "Gay It Forward" principle and take Barry on as their protégé, shaping him into a fabulous gay man. Jack and Will start Barry's transformation by focusing on the important stuff: hair, body, and gay bar skills. Barry finds the process insulting and demeaning until he realizes he will never bone up on being gay (or bone a gay, for that matter!) if he doesn't tone up first.

Grace realizes Will has a crush on Fagmalion Barry

but, of course, Will denies it. But later, when Will sees Barry at the Human Rights Campaign gala, he goes gaga over the fully transformed, attractive, and, finally, beardless man. Naturally Jack develops a crush on Barry, too. Jack beats Will to the punch, and asks Barry out first. Will and Jack compete for Barry's affections, but Will eventually wins. Sadly, their relationship quickly unravels when Barry expresses his desire to see other people, play the field, and explore his new life as an out gay man.

Vince D'Angelo, played by Bobby Cannavale

Italian cop and accessories enthusiast, Vince is Will's first long-term boyfriend on the series and ultimately becomes the man with whom Will spends the rest of his life.

When Will first meets Police Officer Vince D'Angelo in Season 6's "Courting Disaster," the pair do not seem destined to be anything but adversaries. While Will is teaching Karen how to drive, Vince pulls them over for speeding. When Will discovers Vince forgot to sign Karen's ticket, he decides to challenge the hot cop in traffic court. After Will announces his name for the judge, Vince realizes that Will is the guy their mutual friends Joe and Larry have been trying to set him up with. Their chemistry instantly changes, and Karen brokers a date for them in exchange for dropping the charges.

Will and Vince start off strong but when Vince is fired from the police force for trying on cashmere gloves during an armed robbery, he sinks into depression.

Vince and Will mutually decide to "take a break," which both men know really means "break up."

Will doesn't see Vince again until Season 8 when he runs into him working undercover as a waiter. Will realizes he made a mistake, but nothing happens until Vince attends Will's father's funeral a few episodes later. The reunion makes them realize they are still in love. In the series finale, their relationship continues for many years and they adopt a son, Ben, who marries Grace and Leo's daughter, Lila.

James Hanson, played by Taye Diggs

In Season 8's "Von Trapped," Will does what any single gay man in the city would do: He dresses as Captain Von Trapp to attend a "Sound of Music Sing-Along" with Grace. When Will accidentally goes to the wrong theater he meets James Hanson, a smoking hot Taye Diggs. The two have an instant connection, but no numbers are exchanged. Later, Will assumes their encounter meant more to Will than it did to James. The episode ends with James looking for Will at the "Sound of Music" theater after Will's left.

As luck would have it, Will and James are destined to be a couple . . . at least for three more episodes. In "I Love L. Gay," Will runs into James at a hotel in Los Angeles and they instantly re-spark until James reveals he's Canadian and will be deported in four days. After seeing how happy James makes Will, Grace offers to marry James so he can stay in the country and give a relationship with Will a chance. In the next episode, "The Definition of Marriage," Karen throws a huge wedding ceremony for Grace and James. At the end of the wedding, Will and James sing Stevie Wonder to each other, every bit the loving couple. All that changes in the next episode, "Expectations," when James reveals increasingly unappealing qualities to Will, like his fondness for stealing cabs from old ladies in the rain. Will tells Grace to annul the marriage.

The Girlfriends of Will Truman

Claire, played by Megyn Price

Claire and Will dated in high school. He describes her to Jack as the "Grace before [he] met Grace." Claire reconnects with Will in Season 2 to ask Will for a sperm donation. She's single, she wants a baby, and she wants it to be his. Will nearly goes through with it, but changes his mind when he realizes if he is to give his sperm to any woman, he wants it to be Grace.

Diane, played by Mira Sorvino

Diane is the woman Will slept with after he broke up with Grace. She's also the only woman he ever slept with, and marked his final attempt at trying to be straight. She's *also* Leo's ex-girlfriend. In Season 6 Diane shows up at Leo and Grace's dinner party and Diane reveals that sex with Will was the only time she ever had an orgasm. (She came close with Leo once in a public bathroom, but Ed Koch walked on in them and ruined the moment.) After her admission, everyone is uncomfortable, most of all Will.

The Boyfriends of Grace Adler

Danny, played by Tom Verica

Grace and Danny dated for two years before the "Pilot" episode. Will never felt that Danny was right for Grace. For Will, Danny's habit of high-fiving Grace after sex pretty much summed up the weaknesses of his character. Grace leaves Danny at the altar in "The Pilot," but they rekindle their romance at the end of Season 1. Grace and Danny don't last long but his resurfacing makes Will and Grace realize that since Grace moved in with Will, neither has moved on from their respective breakups. Danny isn't seen again until Season 4's "Dying Is Easy, Comedy Is Hard," when Grace forces Will to be her date to Danny's wedding. While talking up Danny to his jittery bride, Grace panics that she made the wrong decision in dumping him years earlier. However, the feeling quickly passes.

Josh, played by Corey Parker

Grace dated Josh, a gentle New Age vegetarian, while she was dating Ben, Will's boss. In the Season 3 premiere, "New Will City," Grace anguishes over which man she should choose to date exclusively. Ultimately the decision is made for her when Jack and Josh hook up.

Ben Doucette, played by Gregory Hines

Ben is first introduced as a nonpaying client of Grace's midway through Season 2 in "Terms of Employment." Grace tries to sue Ben for breaking their contract, but when Ben offers Will a job, things gets complicated. At first Ben seems ruthless and immoral, doing whatever it takes to get ahead and make money, but he can also be charming and, thanks to the talents of Gregory Hines, is one hell of a tap dancer. Will urges Grace to make nice with Ben at a dinner Will hosts. Things get nicer than Will intended, and Ben and Grace end up sleeping together. They date until Season 3's "Grace 0, Jack 2000," when Ben dumps Grace after she debates dumping him. They both agree that while their relationship is nice, it will never go anywhere because they are not in love.

Mark, played by Ken Marino

Grace and Mark meet in Season 3's "Three's a Crowd, Six Is a Freakshow." Grace dumps Mark as soon as she finds out he has six toes.

Nicholas, played by Jeremy Piven

Grace dated Nicholas, a cellist with the Boston Symphony, for six weeks sometime in the nineties. Their relationship was tumultuous, but they had great chemistry. In Season 3's "Love Plus One," Nicholas pops back into town and wants to meet up with Grace, who assumes sex is his motivation. She's right—but Nicholas wants to have a threesome with Grace and his current girlfriend. Grace tries to go through with it, but ultimately decides she's not a threesome kind of girl.

Nathan, played by Woody Harrelson

Nathan first meets Grace in Season 3's "The Young and the Tactless" when he removes her wet laundry from the dryer. Grace storms up to his apartment and they argue while Nathan makes a mix-tape for his girlfriend: "Heavy Metal Songs of Love and Devotion." When Grace mocks Nathan's attempts to repair his troubled relationship, Nathan suggests that Grace isn't one to dole out the love advice since she is single and living with a gay man. Over the next few days, Grace repeatedly knocks on his door, continuing their argument. After days of being yelled at by Grace, Nathan realizes he likes her and asks her out. At first the two date secretly, as Grace is ashamed of Nathan's boorish ways, knowing Will would never approve. The sneaking around doesn't last long, though. As soon as Grace finds out Nathan is sharing Apartment 12C with his now ex-girlfriend, she has him move in with her and Will.

Will and Nathan clash, but Nathan eventually wins him over. The real trouble starts when Nathan wants to push things to the next level with Grace. Grace worries if she ends up with sloppy, carefree Nathan they'll live in a mud hut in Tarrytown and she'll be shopping at the local K-mart. Grace even plans a trip to Morocco with Will to avoid Nathan. Will calls her out on her behavior, saying: "I just don't want you using me as an excuse for not getting on with your life."

Declaring their love for each other, Grace and Nathan reunite but soon Nathan feels that Grace always puts Will's needs before his. A shopping trip to Barney's quickly solves this problem: Nathan realizes he needs Will to meet Grace's needs that fall outside his area of expertise (and patience), like picking out dresses for five hours. Nathan and Grace's relationship ultimately hits the skids when he proposes to her during sex. Grace is upset that Nathan would propose under such unromantic circumstances and makes him take the question "off the table." Will convinces her she's made a mistake, and she decides to ask Nathan to marry her. He breaks up with her instead, saying that although he loves her, he finds their relationship too difficult.

Dr. Marvin "Leo" Markus, played by Harry Connick, Jr.

QUOTE

"Don't break [Will]. I still need him for the 20 percent of you I can't handle."

—Leo Markus to Grace Adler

By the end of Season 4, Grace has given up on meeting the handsome (preferably Jewish) prince on a white horse. Instead, she decides to have a baby with Will.

When Leo, the Southern-born Jewish doctor, meets Grace, he not only turns her world upside down, but he wreaks havoc on Will's plans as well. On the morning Leo enters Grace's life, Will's sperm is scheduled to depart for Grace's uterus via artificial insemination. On her way to the clinic, Grace runs through Central

Park and collides with a lamppost. She comes to as
Leo, riding a white horse, reaches to help her. Leo, on
horseback, drops Grace off in front of the clinic, but
before he leaves he asks her out. She declines because
of her plans with Will, even though Leo seems the perfect catch: handsome, Jewish, doctor . . . Grace leaves,
saying, "I gotta go before I find out you come from
money."

But Leo pursues Grace ardently and she finally gives
in. After a whirlwind two-month romance, the duo decide to get married when they run into Katie Couric
conducting a mass wedding in Central Park. Their
marriage starts out rocky, with Grace worried she
rushed into the union and also struggling to achieve
the proper balance between the two men in her life: her
husband and her best friend. Fortunately, unlike Grace's
previous boyfriends, Leo enjoys and supports Grace's
intimacy with Will. Just when Leo and Grace find their
groove as Old Marrieds, Leo receives word he's been
chosen to serve in Africa with Doctors Without
Borders—his lifelong dream. Leo's service abroad in
various countries without Grace tests the strength of
their marriage. In a moment of weakness, Leo cheats
on Grace with a doctor in Cambodia. Unable to forgive
him despite his efforts to make it up to her, Grace seeks
a divorce in the beginning of Season 7. Grace dates
other men for the rest of the series, but ultimately Leo
is her great love.

In the fifth episode of Season 8, " Love Is in the Airplane," Leo and Grace bump into each other on a red-
eye to London and join the mile-high club. Their roll in
the airplane leaves Grace pregnant. When Grace hears

that Leo is in town, she works up the nerve to tell him about the baby and her feelings for him. Unfortunately, Leo has met someone else and is planning to get remarried. Grace decides to let him move on with his life and stays quiet about her bun in the oven. Months later, Leo returns to New York to tell Grace he loves her and wants to marry her, have babies with her, and grow old together. Leo and Grace move to Rome for two years, where Grace gives birth to their daughter, Lila. Eventually, Grace and Leo move back to Brooklyn and, years later, Lila and Will's son, Ben, fall in love and get married.

Nick, played by Ed Burns

Nick is a greeting-card designer Grace meets in Season 7's "Dance Cards and Greeting Cards." Nick is attending a Valentine's Day party in Grace's office building when he stops at Grace Adler designs by mistake. In

QUOTE

"I like to think that long after the finale airs, Leo and Grace go on and they live a very, very happy life together with their little family."

—Harry Connick, Jr., in a 2006 interview with *People* magazine

the next episode, "The Birds and the Bees," Grace asks Will to join them on her first date with Nick because she's afraid of throwing herself at him and ruining their chance at a relationship. The date ends with appropriate kissing (and cab ride boob grabbing as a reward for telling Grace she's pretty), and Nick asks Grace out again. Their romance blooms until Out TV buys Nick's screenplay. The project forces Nick to relocate to Vancouver.

Tom Cassidy, played by Eric Stoltz

Tom and Grace dated her senior year of college. She thought he was very romantic, as he would always make sure his roommate was asleep before they did it. When

THE GAY BOYFRIENDS OF GRACE ADLER

"Oh, my God. I've turned another one."

—Grace Adler

WILL: They dated in college. She was the last girl-friend he had before coming out.

JOSH: Dated Grace until he felt the lusty call of Jack.

JAMES: Although technically not her boyfriend, Grace married Will's squeeze James so that he wouldn't be deported.

JUST ANOTHER RANDOM GAY BOYFRIEND: A guy she once dated in a rock band ended up as a chorus boy on the *Queen Mary II*.

Tom calls Grace out of the blue in Season 7's "Friends with Benefits," Grace assumes Tom is interested in getting back together. Those dreams are quickly dashed when Tom arrives at Grace's office with his wife, Viv (Bridgette Flannery). Tom and Viv bought a hotel and want Grace to do the interior design. Tom makes advances toward Grace, so she quits the job. However, their chemistry is too strong to deny, and Grace finds herself very tempted. In Season 8's premiere episode, "Alive and Schticking," Jack convinces Grace that she's a woman "of quality" and cannot go through with the affair.

The Not-So-Many Boyfriends of Jack McFarland

QUOTE

"Jack, if I'm supposed to stay away from every guy you've ever slept with, that would leave me with . . . women."

—Will

Stuart, played by Dave Foley
Stuart is first introduced in Season 6's "Ice Cream Balls" as Will's client. He is the CEO of "Stuff I Invented in

My Garage Industries." Stuart tells Will he wants a date with Jack, but Jack only agrees to the date when Will bribes him with a ChapStick and pocket change. Despite the lack of initial heat, after only one date Jack becomes smitten with Stuart. The two date and nearly move in together, but back out of the arrangement, thinking they're moving too fast. Still they are going strong when Jack runs into Stuart at a movie theater with a younger man. Jack panics, thinking Stuart is having an affair. Stuart reveals that back in college he "experimented with heterosexuality" and had a son. Unfortunately their relationship ends when Jack cheats on Stuart.

Beverly Leslie, played by Leslie Jordan

Beverly Leslie, Karen's campy, Southern, pint-sized nemesis, is a gay man who goes to great lengths to hide his sexual orientation among the high-society circle of friends he shares with Karen. Beverly's spouse, Krystal, is extremely wealthy and never seen. Beverly first appears in Season 3 when he tries to woo Rosario away from Karen—the first of many underhanded moves.

Though Beverly tries to appear straight by denouncing homosexuality, he brings Benji, a strapping black "business associate," to most social affairs. Jack describes them as the "most stable in-the-closet, short-tall, black-white, young-old, disgusting-hot couple" he knows. Karen takes pleasure in constantly trying to get Beverly to out himself at public gatherings. Benji dumps Beverly sometime before the series finale. Beverly approaches Jack to be his new "business associate." Jack is revolted by the idea, but Karen, whose fortune is wiped out, pressures Jack to be Beverly's concubine so that Jack can financially support Karen the way she did for him over the years. When Jack says he can't do it, Karen tells him what he needs to make it through the experience: "You'll do it the same way any other self-respecting woman does. Get on your back, point your heels to Jesus, and think of handbags." Before they can consummate their union, Karen intervenes, telling Jack she can't let him go through with it. Jack, now the sole ben-

Q FACT

Leslie Jordan won an Emmy for Outstanding Guest Actor in a Comedy Series in 2006 for his portrayal of Beverly Leslie.

LESLIE JORDAN ON BEVERLY LESLIE

My agent called me and said, 'Do you still have that little white linen suit that John Ritter gave you?' (When I did *Hearts Afire*, a Linda Bloodworth Thomason series, John Ritter gave me this adorable white linen suit.) My agent said put on that little white suit and run over to *Will & Grace*. They're looking for Truman Capote–esque. The character was already named Beverly Leslie. And it was not written for me! It happened so quickly that I didn't even have a script ahead of time. I show up in a white suit and pick up the sides [scripts] and it says a tiny man with a southern accent in a white suit. I don't even remember auditioning. They just said, 'You're it!'

Being from the South, I immediately knew that character. Especially around the Baptist churches, there are

eficiary of Beverly's fortune, is saved from the awkwardness of a breakup when a strong wind blows Beverly off the balcony. With Beverly's death, Jack in-

always these obviously homosexual men who are married and I don't know if they have little nocturnal escapades or what, but you just think, 'Honey, you're gay!' When I read the script and saw that I was going to have a black boyfriend that I was to introduce as my 'business associate,' I fell on the floor.

During rehearsal Max said, 'Quit making him so nelly or quit making him so effeminate.' And then Jimmy Burrows runs over to me and says, 'What did Max tell you?' I said 'I think Max wants me to calm him down a little bit.' Jimmy says, 'Don't listen to him!' and runs back out. I thought the joke was that Beverly Leslie was so obviously homosexual. What Max was doing was trying to get me to a level of reality. You could be broad on that show, but it always, always had to be anchored in reality.

—Leslie Jordan ("Beverly Leslie")

herits everything. As for poor Benji, who put the better part of his youth into being Beverly's business associate, he gets nothing.

Beverly Leslie's drink is a B-52 with one ice cube, though he's also been known to enjoy a blackberry julep with a baby aspirin chaser.

Karen Walker's Boudoir

Stanley Walker, unseen

"I am a married woman. Sure, my husband is an enormous bulldozer of a man who has to be hit with a stun gun before he can be weighed or medicated, but when I said yes to his attorneys, I meant that to be forever."

—Karen Walker

"He was this grotesque 900-pound figure who Karen loves. To actually see him would've ruined something."

—David Kohan, Series Co-Creator

Karen's third husband and great love, Stanley Walker, is never seen on-screen (except for his hand in "New Will City"). Stan is an obese, hairy billionaire who wears a giant toupee and has a bad case of recurring psoriasis. Despite his physical shortcomings, Karen loves him dearly for most of the series. A flashback in Season 3's "Lows in the Mid-Eighties" reveals that Karen was in love with Stan ten years before their marriage in 1995. She even passed up romantic opportunities with a sultan and Martina Navratilova to be with him. Stan was married at the time and has two children, Mason and Olivia, from his previous marriage to a woman named Kathy.

Stan and Karen's marriage takes a turn for the worse when Stan goes to prison for tax evasion in Season 4. While in the clink, he has an affair with a tarty English cafeteria worker named Lorraine Finster (Minnie Driver). The affair continues after his release, and Karen accidentally walks in on them having sex. Karen leaves Stan but continues to have strong feelings for him ... and his money. Stan dies suddenly at the end of Season 5,

QUOTE

"Dab of roast beef behind each knocker."

—Lorraine Finster, on Stan's favorite perfume

leaving Karen a widow. But at the end of Season 7, Stan contacts Will and reveals that he faked his death because he had landed himself in hot water with the mob. Karen eventually finds out that Stan is alive and is too hurt to take him back. The two divorce by the end of Season 8. It turns out that everything Stanley had was borrowed, and Karen ends up with nothing.

Lionel Banks, played by Rip Torn

QUOTE

"Finally a man who knows how to make a woman feel like a girl, and how to make that girl feel like a slut, and how to make that slut feel like a woman."

—Karen Walker, on Lionel Banks

Karen first meets the smooth-talking charmer Lionel Banks in Season 4's finale, "A.I.: Artificial Insemination." Upset about Stanley's extended prison sentence, Karen drowns her sorrows at a hotel bar with her favorite bartender, Smitty. Lionel overhears her laugh and makes his move. Karen enjoys flirting with him under the alias Anastasia Beaverhousen. Lionel continues to pursue Karen despite her confession that she is actually not the single Miss Beaverhousen but the married Mrs. Walker. Karen can't resist Lionel's lure and they do "everything but." When Karen decides to finally sleep with Lionel, Stanley surprises her by getting out of prison early. Karen realizes she has to break it off with Lionel for the sake of Stanley, but still finds herself unable to resist him. She sends Rosario to break up with him for her, but Rosario can't resist him either and they end up in bed. Karen finally breaks up with Lionel, saying that Stan is her only love.

Lyle Finster, played by John Cleese

When Karen thinks she's tracked down Lorraine Finster, Stanley's mistress, at the Hotel Knickerbocker, she's surprised to learn "L. Finster" is actually Lorraine's father, Lyle. Lyle woos Karen, but she wants nothing to do with him aside from occasional ravenous smooching. Everything changes when Lorraine tells Karen to stay away from her father. Karen jumps into bed with Lyle and arranges for Lorraine to walk in on them. Lyle chooses Karen over Lorraine—a gesture that makes Karen realize she's in love with him. The two marry in Vegas at a big wedding featuring a performance by Jennifer Lopez. However, their bliss is short-lived. Lyle makes too many "executive decisions" about the wedding and Karen's life, like forcing her to fund his traveling puppet theater against her wishes. During his toast Lyle says he's lucky to have found "a woman who's happy to mortgage her entire personal identity" for him. With that, Karen announces she wants a divorce.

Artemus Johnson, played by Will Arnett

Karen and Artemus, who appears in Episode 2 of Season 7, "Back Up, Dancer," met at Seattle's Space Needle in 1992. They made love in the rain and enjoyed activities like taking the monorail to Seahawks and Sonics games, watching them throw fish at Pike Place Market, and sipping lattes at the original Starbucks. When Karen runs into Artemus at Jack's audition to be Janet Jackson's backup dancer, the heat's still there and they get back together. Karen, in love with Artemus, even begs Jack to throw a "dance-off" so that Artemus can remain on Janet's squad. Jack reluctantly steps aside for Artemus, who turns around and dumps Karen, having gotten what he needed. But Janet decides she wants four dancers instead of five, and Artemus is cut from the crew. Artemus claims to be both very young and very old, but he has a daughter who recently graduated from law school.

Scott Woolley, played by Jeff Goldblum

Scott went to high school with Karen back in the days when she was flat-chested and had her sights set on becoming senior class president instead of a boozy trophy wife. Scott Woolley was her opponent and would have won, had Karen not suddenly developed her signature bosom and nabbed all the votes. Neither one of them was ever the same again. Woolley decided to take vengeance on Karen and in Season 7's "Board Games," he tries to sneak his way into the presidency of Walker, Inc. Karen thwarts his efforts by threatening to expose the Walker, Inc., board members' dirty laundry. Still stinging from their last encounter, Woolley pops up again, using the alias Mr. Osment, to offer Grace an opportunity to design a new restaurant, but only if she fires Karen. Grace and Karen figure out the ruse. Later, Grace suggests to Woolley that his Karen obsession may have more to do with Woolley's attraction to her than wanting to destroy her. In the next episode, "Dance Cards and Greeting Cards," Woolley sends Karen flowers and candy for Valentine's Day but she dismisses the gifts. Besides, she's already met a new fat love on the Internet whose e-mail address is ElevatorHazard@whalewatcher.com. Later, Woolley reveals that he is really Karen's on-line boyfriend. Touched by Woolley's genuine affection for her, Karen lets him down gently after allowing him a quick feel of her boobs.

Malcom Widmark, played by Alec Baldwin

Malcolm is a shadowy government agent who helped Stan fake his death. For two years, Malcolm and Stanley lived together in seclusion somehow under the auspices of *Big Brother,* the television show. Malcolm meets Will at the end of Season 7 pretending to be an admirer of Will's writing. After Malcolm's "friends" at *The New Yorker* pass on one of Will's essays, Malcolm offers Will a job as a lawyer at his charitable organization. Will jumps at the opportunity, but soon grows suspicious. In the

Season 7 finale, "Kiss and Tell," Will discovers Stanley is alive and the whole thing has been a setup.

When Malcolm first meets Karen, he is enamored both by her beauty and her breasts, which he hopes to one day see coming toward him on a "very bumpy road." The two date until Season 8's "Steams Like Old Times." After Karen hears that Stan gave Malcolm his blessing to date Karen and put up no fight whatsoever, Karen runs back to her lovable fatty and leaves Malcolm in the dust.

Sean Hayes

Sean Hayes, born on June 26, 1970, in the Chicago suburb of Glen Ellyn, Illinois, is a man of many talents. A gifted musician, he studied performance and conducting at Illinois State University. In the early days of his career, he supported himself as a classical pianist. After college, Sean studied theater in Chicago, where he performed with the famed Second City comedy troupe and enjoyed a successful career as a commercial actor. But before long he moved to Los Angeles for a chance at television and film roles.

Sean caught the attention of Hollywood when he starred in the gay romantic comedy, "Billy's Hollywood Screen Kiss," which was a big hit at Sundance. *Will & Grace* was Sean's first pilot. Jack turned out to be a career-defining role, earning Sean an Emmy for Outstanding Supporting Actor in a Comedy Series in 2000.

While Jack is quick to brag about his sexual exploits, Sean likes to keep his personal life to himself. He's never admitted to being gay or straight, which has caused some controversy. "I love that people think I'm gay," he said in an interview with *Entertainment Weekly*. "I love that people think I'm straight. I think it's fun." Sean wants to avoid labels so his characters won't be looked upon with preconceived notions. "There are some actors who, the second you ask them if they're playing a gay role, they say, 'I'm straight! I'm straight and I'm married. I have two kids and I'm straight. Did I mention

I'm straight? I'm straight,'" he told *Entertainment Weekly.* "Wouldn't it be great if they didn't say that? Then you might actually believe they're gay."

In addition to his award-winning turn as Jack McFarland, Sean has appeared on the small screen in *Scrubs, 30 Rock, Campus Ladies,* and *Lovespring International,* produced by his *Will & Grace* co-star Eric McCormack. Sean was most recently seen in Rob Reiner's *The Bucket List,* starring Jack Nicholson and Morgan Freeman.

CHAPTER FIVE

Thicker Than Evian: The Families of Will, Grace, Jack, and Karen

The Trumans of Connecticut

QUOTE

> "I like Will's family. They drink."
>
> —Karen

Marilyn Truman, played by Blythe Danner
Marilyn, the matriarch of Will's Connecticut family, is an ardent fan of alcohol and Lladro statues. Her dislikes include musicals (especially ones about "the poor") and her husband's affair.

Marilyn makes her first appearance in Season 4's

"Moveable Feast." Will's father, George (Sydney Pollack), is away on a "business trip" (WASP code for boinking the mistress), and Marilyn must host Thanksgiving without him. Although Marilyn has her own affairs, George's relationship with his mistress, Tina (Leslie Ann Warren), causes Marilyn great heartache. Marilyn leaves George, but a chance encounter leads Mr. and Mrs. Truman to make "pookie pookie" again. Marilyn decides Tina is a necessary part of her marriage with George, and the women work out a time-share arrangement behind Will's back.

Will has issues with the way both of his parents have treated his homosexuality. In Season 8's "A Little Christmas Queer," Will is offended when Marilyn makes a fuss over the Christmas show put on by Will's nephew, the undeniably gay nine-year-old, Jordie. Growing up, Marilyn always ruined Will's shows "doing anything to distract the family from watching her gay son do fan kicks in the beanbag chair." When Will storms out of Jordie's Spectacular, Marilyn confronts him, revealing that she knows she messed up with him and was hoping to do better by Jordie. Ultimately Marilyn is a supportive mother who is very proud of Will.

Q FACT

Marilyn's drink is "The Blue Marilyn" (Blue Curacao, vodka, a splash of peach schnapps, some bitters, a pinch of sugar, and melted cherry Sucrets).

George Truman, Will's father, played by Sydney Pollack

Unlike Will's mother, Will's father, George, displays very few affects of WASP society. But like Marilyn and the rest of Will's family, George doesn't like addressing his affair in the open, choosing instead to avoid the topic altogether or refer to his mistress, Tina, as a colleague. Grace, baffled by the Trumans' behavior, has sometimes felt like a "Jewish Jane Goodall" to their "Goyim in the Mist."

Although George loves his son, he has a difficult time accepting Will's homosexuality. In 1985, when Will told his father he was gay, George drove his car into a tree. Over the years he seemed to accept Will, and the two enjoyed a warm relationship. But in George's first appearance in Season 2, Will learns that George has been telling his co-workers that Will and Grace are married. After Will confronts George, George corrects his mistake by outing Will in an embarrassing speech, declaring his pride for his gay son. Over the next few years, their main conflicts have more to do with George's "business associate," Tina, than with Will's sexual orientation. However, George's concerns with Will's homosexuality reappear in Season 8's "A Blanket Apology" when George gives Will's baby blanket to Grace. Will is offended because he doesn't believe that George expects his gay son to have children. George insists that he's never been ashamed of Will, but ultimately admits he'd "prefer" if Will weren't gay. Will storms out and over the next few days refuses to take George's calls. Finally, Will picks up the phone only to learn that his Dad has had a heart attack and passed away.

Sam Truman, played by John Slattery (Season 1) and Steven Weber (Season 8)

No matter who plays Sam Truman, the character of Will's brother and Grace always have chemistry. Sam is the version of Will that Grace can sleep with. Will first mentions Sam in "The Pilot." Will and his brother haven't spoken for five years because Will called Sam's then fiancée (current ex) "morose, controlling, and icy." As a result Sam cut Will out of his life. Sam makes his first appearance in Episode 14 of Season 1, "Big Brother Is Coming." Grace forces a surprise reunion for the brothers who, after a long night of arguing, make some headway in repairing their relationship. But the peace quickly ends when Grace sleeps with Sam. Will doesn't want Sam with Grace because she's "his"—a concept that upsets both Grace and Sam. Later Will apologizes, admitting that Grace should date whomever she wants. Ultimately, Grace decides her relationship with Will is more important than a potential romance with Sam.

Sam doesn't appear again until Season 8. The gang goes to Will's family's house for Christmas, and Grace and Sam have an awkward reunion, which quickly leads to making out in the attic while "looking for the menorah." Sam's divorce has finally gone through and he wants to start a relationship with Grace right away, but she senses Sam's rush to dating is inspired by fear of being single rather than pure Grace love. Sam concedes that Grace may be right, and they part amicably.

Jordan Truman, played by Reed Alexander

Jordan "Jordie" Truman is Sam's adopted son and Will's nephew. For a nine-year-old, Jordie is comfortable with his flamboyant side. His stage name is Jordan St. James. One Halloween, he went as Lynda Carter (not Wonder Woman), and he's created a new cologne scent he calls Scoundrel. It's generally accepted that Jordie is gay.

Paul Truman, Will's brother, played by Jon Tenney

Will's brother Paul appears in Season 4 at the Truman family Thanksgiving celebration. Will and Paul are very different, although they both want to be their mother's favorite. Paul feels Will made a "choice" to be gay and sees Will's lifestyle as less valid than his own. Will doesn't much care for Paul.

Peggy Truman, played by Helen Slater

Peggy, Paul's wife and Will's sister-in-law, makes a brief appearance alongside Paul. Mostly, she tries to keep Grace away from her husband, fearing Grace will try to sleep with him since she slept with Will's other brother, Sam. Of course, her fears are unfounded.

Tina, played by Leslie Ann Warren

Tina, George Truman's bubbly, slightly dimwitted mistress, first appears in Season 3. Grace catches Tina and George together at *Seussical the Musical*. George tries to pass Tina off as a "colleague" to Grace, and later to Will, with little success. Later in Season 4, Will and Grace try to fix Tina up with someone else to get her away from George, but their plan fails when the only available suitor is gay Larry. Naturally, Marilyn and Tina hate each other, but over the years they come to an understanding about sharing George.

They last see each other at George's funeral, where they share a hug.

Grace's Mishpucheh

QUOTE

"We took a train up to my parent's house in Schenectady, where Will learned the answer to that age-old question, 'Whatever did happen to Baby Jane?'"

—Grace, on her mother

Bobbi Adler, played by Debbie Reynolds
Grace's mother, Bobbi Adler, is an actress, singer, and frequent player on the stages of Schenectady, New York. Unfortunately for Grace, Bobbi never turns off the chorus girl charm, often breaking into song and dance, embarrassing her daughter. Bobbi also has the buttinsky qualities of a typical Jewish mother, always trying to set Grace and her friends up on (usually horrible) dates. Bobbi spends a lot of time with her swishy arranger, Julius, whom she's known for many years. Grace

is often frustrated by Bobbi's need to be the center of attention.

Bobbi's first appearance is in Season 1's "The Unsinkable Mommy Adler," when she swoops into town suggesting that Will and Grace get married because the "sex thing" dies anyway. Will says he wouldn't marry Grace even if he were straight. When Grace presses Will for a reason, he explains that Grace, like her mother, needs to be the center of attention in her relationships. At first Grace is deeply offended but comes to accept that Will may be right. Grace grows weary of Bobbi's criticism and meddling when it comes to her appearance and love life, but ultimately they have a strong, caring relationship.

Martin Adler, played by Alan Arkin

Grace often wishes her dad, Martin, were warmer and more attentive. Grace feels Martin hasn't noticed any of her achievements since she was twelve and accidentally let the cat out. Martin is often in front of the television watching *Kojak*. He once missed Grace's field hockey finals because Rosie Grier was signing autographs at the local Ford dealership.

Q FACT

Bobbi sometimes performs a dance called the "I told you so" dance. Grace isn't a fan.

Martin only appears in Season 7 when Grace visits him for his birthday. She encourages Martin to treat her as something other than a punchline. He tells her he loves her and then with great effort tries to force a conversation about her life. That's over quickly and the two of them laugh at Grace's awkwardness in the chair she's sitting in.

Janet Adler, Grace's older sister, played by Geena Davis

QUOTE

"You are the screw-up older sister. Joyce is the heavy younger sister. And I am the perfect one in the middle. I am the glue that holds you two losers together."

—Grace, to her sister Janet

Janet, Grace's "screw-up older sister," surprises Grace (whom she calls "Smudge") with a visit in Season 6's "The Accidental Tsuris." Janet comes to town to launch her jewelry business on a folding table at St. Mark's Place, where she expects to gain celebrity clientele. Grace challenges Janet to get a real job and her own apartment. But when Janet lands a job at Lord and

Taylor and a new studio apartment, Grace worries that her status as the normal Adler sister will be challenged. Eventually, Janet reveals her new life is a sham fabricated by Will, and the two sisters rejoice at Janet's enduring loserdom.

Joyce Adler, Grace's younger sister, played by Sara Rue

Grace's younger sister, Joyce, only appears in Season 3's "Lows in the Mid-Eighties." In the 80s she wore a retainer and attended Camp Yes-I-Can, where she drew unicorns. When Joyce first meets Will, she's jealous of Grace's hot boyfriend. After Will comes out in front of the whole Adler family, Joyce yells at Grace for "ruining everything." Joyce has a problem with stress eating.

Julius

While not technically family, Julius, Bobbi Adler's excessively refined musical "arranger," is part of the Adler clan. When Julius first meets a collegiate Will in 1985 at the Adler home, he instantly recognizes him as a fellow gay man. When Will announces his impending marriage to Grace, Julius tells Will he's been engaged twice, suggesting that Julius has been through a charade (or two) in his day.

Karen's Nearest and Not Always Dearest

QUOTE

> "Santa Maria. It has a mother?"
>
> —Rosario, upon learning about Karen's mother

Lois Whitely, played by Suzanne Pleshette

Lois is Karen's con-woman, lowlife mother who calls Karen "Kiki." Over the years Karen has sent her mom a check once a month to keep her as far from Karen as possible, which turns out to mean an Irish bar in Yonkers. Jack, thinking he's doing a good thing, reunites Karen with her estranged mother in Season 4. Karen had a hard life with her mother, always moving from town to town as part of Lois's scams. When Lois and Karen reunite, Lois asks Karen to do just one more job, which lands Karen in a hideous outfit, pretending to be retarded to bilk a geezer out of his money.

Lois isn't seen again until Season 6, when she moves

back to the city. She hires Grace to renovate her apartment for a limited budget, forcing Grace, Karen, and Rosario to do all the manual labor. When they finish, Lois decides to flip the apartment and realize her life-long dream of owning a McDonald's in Tokyo.

Sister Gin, played by Bernadette Peters

When Karen and her sister, Gin, were younger, they played a game of Twister on top of a rickety old saw mill. Full of jealousy, they each secretly loosened a floorboard so the other would fall through. Gin, a dancer, was the one who fell and broke her ankle. As a result, her left leg is 3/8 of an inch shorter than her right. Karen feels so guilty she supports Gin, paying her $300,000 a month until Season 8's "Whatever Happened to Baby Gin?" when Stan has cut her off.

Mason Walker, unseen

Mason Walker shares two important qualities with his father: he's fat and never seen on the show. Mason is often referred to as "the fat one," and his zest for food suggests he may end up as big as his famously fat father one day.

Olivia Walker, played by Hallee Hirsch

Karen has expressed her love for stepdaughter Olivia in her own way, such as paying for the early-nineties TGIF television show, *Step by Step*, to remain in production two extra seasons because it was Olivia's favorite. While they've never been close, Karen and Olivia have had some fun together, like the time they glued a cookie to the floor and watched Mason get splinters trying to pick it up. Olivia is often alluded to, but her only appearance is in Season 7's "Christmas Break."

Sylvia Walker,
played by Ellen Albertini Dow

Stan's tiny, elderly, fur coat–wearing mother gives Karen the shakes and for "all the wrong reasons." When Karen dumps the old lady on Will and Jack one night, the boys are forced to take Sylvia to a new gay bar. Sylvia is surprisingly helpful in getting Will a date, but when she realizes she's been cruising with "fags" she panics, revealing her extreme homophobia.

The McFarland Clan of Greater New York

Judith McFarland,
played by Veronica Cartwright

Jack's mother, Judith, conceived Jack at a pool party with an anonymous stranger in a Nixon mask. Judith, like Jack, is self-involved. Will says about Judith and Jack: "The fruit didn't fall far from that tree." Her first and only appearance is in Season 2's "Homo for the Holidays." Will invites Judith to join the gang for Thanksgiving. When she arrives it becomes clear that Jack never told her he was gay. At dinner he finally outs himself. Judith has no problem with it and tells Jack he could never disappoint her. After Jack's revelation, Judith confesses that Daniel McFarland is not Jack's real father.

Daniel McFarland, played by Beau Bridges

QUOTE

"You were a tough kid to figure out. It was like having a foreign exchange student in the house. You spoke your own language and wore a beret."

—Daniel McFarland, to Jack

Daniel's only appearance is in Season 4's "Moveable Feast." Jack, Elliot, Karen, Will, and Grace visit Daniel as part of their Thanksgiving circuit. Daniel immediately bonds with his grandson, Elliot, a fellow football fan. Their instant connection causes Jack to storm off. Jack returns later and the two men discuss their relationship. Daniel admits he was a "crap father" but wants to get to know Jack now.

Jack's BioDad
An anonymous stranger in a Nixon mask who had sex with Judith in a pool at a key party.

Elliot, played by Michael Angarano
When Jack was seventeen, he donated some of his swimmers to a sperm bank in the New York Family Clinic.

Q QUIZ:
HOW GOOD IS
YOUR *WILL & GRACE*
PYRAMID?

1. Will's one-night stand on Fire Island

   a. Things he regrets
   b. Latin things
   c. Hairy things

2. Grace's Aunt Honey's stomach

   a. Things under moomoos
   b. Things full of kasha
   c. Things that are stapled

3. Professor Gopnick's teeth

   a. Things that are yellow
   b. Things that are missing
   c. Things that are fake

Elliot is the result of Jack's generous submission. Elliot's first appearance is in the Season 3 finale. Elliot, twelve, tracks down Jack, his biological father. At first, Jack rejects the boy, saying that having a son doesn't fit into his "E! True Hollywood Story." Eventually, Jack softens to-

4. Will can't stand him

   a. Frasier Crane
   b. Dennis Miller
   c. Kevin Bacon

5. The postcard Will sent Grace from Italy, or "Everybody Hurts" by R.E.M.

   a. Things that make you sleepy
   b. Things that make you crave garlic
   c. Things that make you cry

6. If Larry ever sees her face again, he'll shoot himself

   a. Paris Hilton
   b. Lindsay Lohan
   c. Tom Cruise

Answers on page 209.

ward Elliot and becomes an involved part of his life. Jack turns out to be a good father to Elliot, and Elliot allows Jack to exhibit his seldom seen less-selfish side. Elliot appears frequently throughout Season 4 and at least once a season for the rest of the series. His last appearance is in Season 8, when Jack and the crew accompany Elliot to L.A. for a college interview.

Bonnie, played by Rosie O'Donnell

Bonnie is Elliot's no-nonsense lesbian mother, who was a nurse at the New York Family Clinic where Jack donated his sperm. Jack's sample was about to go in the trash, so Bonnie stole it and used it on herself.

Having found it difficult to tell Elliot she's gay, Bonnie resents Jack for his ability to be so open with her son about his own sexuality. Her only appearance is in Episode 14 of Season 4, "Dying Is Easy, Comedy Is Hard," when she gets angry with Jack for getting Elliot a "gay haircut" which makes him look "downtown weird." At first Jack thinks Bonnie's rejection of him is due to her intolerance of gay people. When she says she's gay, he doesn't believe her and demands she say something lesbian. She responds with "Home Depot" and Jack is convinced. Eventually Jack wins Bonnie over and she's happy he's a part of Elliot's life. She just wants Jack to keep his haircuts and leather pants to himself.

CHAPTER SIX

The Stars Come Out for Will and Grace

WILL & GRACE, especially in the later seasons, had a reputation for nabbing high-profile guest stars. NBC, like all networks, enjoyed stunt casting and wanted more celebs dropping in on the fab four. Sean was on a softball team with Matt Damon and asked him if he was interested in doing an episode. He was *very* interested. Matt appeared in Season 4's "A Chorus Lie," playing a straight man pretending to be gay to sing in the Manhattan Gay Men's chorus. "Matt Damon was a dream, a doll, so game and self-deprecating," says executive producer Jon Kinnally. Matt even came up with a line mentioning his ex-boyfriend "Ben," a joke about Ben Affleck. As far as mega-wattage celebrities guesting on the show, "Matt Damon opened the floodgates," says Jon.

As *Will & Grace* garnered accolades, Emmys, and ratings, "people started coming to us," says series co-creator David Kohan. Stars and their reps would contact the producers and casting director, Tracy Lilienfield, to express interest. Tracy would "put out the alert to the writers and file it away." Roles were always written first, then they would try to find the right person, she says.

Will & Grace earned a reputation as a fun laboratory

for marquee names to try their hand at sitcoms. After Matt Damon's appearance, Michael Douglas appeared on the show in Season 4's "Fagel Attraction," as a gay detective who concocts a fake sting operation to get closer to Will. "Michael Douglas had a comedy [*The In-Laws*] coming out," says David. "He thought, 'Why not do this show where there is a comedy track record?'" Tracy Lilienfield feels that "there was a period where it was a fun thing to do and it was clear we had big guest stars and we used them well. It wasn't outrageous to ask anyone." Jon adds that "by Season 8 we were calling Meryl Streep's people."

While the star power was good for ratings, the show came under a lot of pressure. "The network wanted bigger and bigger," says executive producer Tracy Poust. "Celeb cameos became an expectation for a little while," adds David. But the writers didn't want to insert a random superstar into every episode. "There's something about it that takes you out of the world of the show," says David. "It worked best when we knew we had a story in the works and we had an actor we could use," says Tracy.

Some of the talents that appeared on the *Will & Grace* stage include Matt Damon, Michael Douglas, Glenn Close, Minnie Driver, Cher, Candice Bergen, Kevin Bacon, Sir Elton John, Gene Wilder, Rosanna Arquette, Lily Tomlin, Parker Posey, Madonna, Britney Spears, Joan Collins, Ellen DeGeneres, Jack Black, Demi Moore, Buck Henry, Stewart Townsend, Sharon Stone, Matt Lauer, Katie Couric, James Earl Jones, Patti LuPone, Debbie Harry, Jennifer Lopez, Sandra Bernhard, Barry Manilow . . . the list goes on and on!

The Friends

QUOTE

"God, they're so much work."

—Joe, on Will and Grace

Joe and Larry, played by Jerry Levine and Tim Bagley

Joe and Larry, notorious party-animal couple turned quiet parents, often serve as a chorus, commenting on the absurd behavior of their friends, Will and Grace. They first appear in Season 3's "Husbands and Trophy Wives" when they invite Will and Jack to their Hamptons home for what the boys assume will be a hot-tubbing, "man-tan reunion." Instead, Joe and Larry have adopted a baby girl, Hannah, and traded clubbing and casual sex for baby bottles and pacifiers. In 2001, Larry and Joe tie the knot at a commitment ceremony in Vermont.

In Season 4's "Whoa, Nelly," Larry gets roped into a date with Will's father's mistress, Tina. Will and Grace have decided that the best way to get Tina out of Mr. Truman's life is to fix her up with someone else. When

TIM BAGLEY ON LARRY

I had worked with one of the *Will & Grace* writers, Kari Lizer, on a show called "Maggie Winters," and she recommended me to the casting director. That's how I got the opportunity to audition for the role of Larry. I just wanted to keep the character simple, and show the normalcy of a gay couple with a baby.

There were a lot of favorite moments. It was a very playful set, and I laughed a lot with the cast. I especially enjoyed the episode 'Whoa, Nellie,' when the writers had Larry go out on a date with Will's father's mistress, played by Leslie Ann Warren. The situation was ridiculous, and so much fun to play

the man Grace lined up cancels, the only replacement they can find on such short notice is Larry. Larry, an enthusiastic fan of needlepoint, has a hard time acting straight and relating to a woman in a romantic way. Will and Grace coach him to treat Tina like his mother, advice that causes Larry to cut Tina's steak for her and monitor her wine intake. Will and Grace think their plan is ruined, but Tina is head over heels. She thinks Larry is wonderful: "He notices everything about me. He's completely honest. He's sensitive, he needlepoints. I love him!"

the discomfort of not knowing how to be on a date with a woman and treating her like my mother. Another favorite moment as Larry was in 'Old Fashioned Piano Party.' Will and Grace were arguing about whether an old fashioned piano party was something real or something Grace just made up, and then I interrupt them to say, 'This is one of the best Old Fashioned Piano Parties I've ever been to.' Then there is an awkward silence and I say, 'I'm uncomfortable and I don't know why,' and I exit. To me that is an example of how good the writing was. You just have to walk in, say a line, then leave, and you get a big laugh.

—Tim Bagley ("Larry")

Rob and Ellen, played by Tom Gallop and Leigh-Allyn Baker

"We might as well make it all the way to the finish line. You know . . . death."

—Ellen, on staying married to Rob

Rob and Ellen, Will and Grace's friends from college, first appear in "The "Pilot" and pop up at least once every season, excluding Season 6. Will and Grace met Rob and Ellen at Columbia back when Will was "straight" and Grace was his girlfriend. Ellen encouraged Grace to sleep with Will when she took him to her parents' house for Thanksgiving in 1985. No longer able to put off sex with Grace, Will realized he was gay and had to come out. Grace and Will didn't talk for a year, but Will maintained a friendship with Rob, who was dating Ellen at the time.

Rob and Ellen, like Joe and Larry, are frequent players at Will and Grace's game nights. Also like Joe and Larry, Ellen and Rob get annoyed by Will and Grace's mastery of Pyramid and their habit of celebrating victories by dancing and screaming, "Suck on it!"

Recurring Characters

Val Basset, played by Molly Shannon
Val can be a lot of fun, but her mental instability makes her a poor choice in friends—a lesson Will and Grace learn repeatedly in Seasons 1 through 7.

Val moves into Apartment 15F in Will and Grace's building in Season 1. At first she seems a charming replacement for Grace, whose busy work schedule has left Will without a partner in crime. Val and Grace do battle for the title of Will's First Hag, but Grace's history with Will and Val's total insanity leaves Val fagless. In Season 2, Val pursues Grace instead of Will. Their friendship quickly ends when Grace discovers Val has stolen her music box. The two women end up coming to blows, and Will has to tear them apart.

Jack has long been an admirer of Val's eccentric ways, but he quickly learns that wingnuts are best enjoyed from afar. In Season 3, Val forces herself into every aspect of Jack's life, even crawling into bed with him and, for Jack, having any woman in his bed (except maybe Karen) is truly traumatic. However, when Val backs off, Jack realizes he misses having a stalker and begs her to come back. She rebuffs him and Jack goes back to being Just Jack.

Val pops up again in Season 4 posing as a designer to compete with Grace. The two women again end up in a brawl, which Karen puts a stop to with a quick karate chop to Val's neck. Val's last appearance shows promise of a new, more stable Val. In Season 7's "One Gay at a Time," Val is in AA and it's changed her life. Grace runs into her at a meeting that Grace crashed for free donuts and therapy. When the truth comes out that Grace is not an alky, just a mooch, Val is outraged. She thinks what Grace did is "awful, and that's coming from a woman who stripped for her father."

Lorraine Finster, played by Minnie Driver

Lorraine Finster, Stan's cockney, prison cafeteria strumpet appears in 6 episodes over seasons 5 and 6. Like Karen, she cares for Stan but also, like Karen, she has a deep and unwavering love for his money. When Stan passes away, Lorraine feels she's earned her right to all of it. But Stan leaves everything to Karen.

Lorraine's campy nature makes her a natural fun friend for Jack but, when forced to choose, he must go to the lady who has the biggest breasts and that is, of

"I was trapped under that fatty for two days. I've got the word 'Posturepedic' permanently imprinted in my spine, and all I get is ''ta'?!"

—Lorraine Finster

course, Karen. However, Jack makes sure to secretly keep on good terms with Lorraine, just in case.

In Season 6, Karen and Lyle Finster, Lorraine's father, have a whirlwind romance that leads to their getting hitched in Vegas. Karen's marriage to "Finny" doesn't last long due to his controlling nature. While Lorraine had no part in their breakup, Karen is relieved that she'll never have to hear the mess hall mistress call her "Mother" ever again.

Nurse Sheila, played by Laura Kightlinger (also a Writer and Consulting Producer for the show)

Nurse Sheila is a bawdy and depressed nurse who works at a sperm bank that has gotten a lot of face time with Will and Grace over the years. First appearing in Season 2, Nurse Sheila is present when Will nearly gives sperm to his high school girlfriend Claire. Later, in Seasons 4 and 5, when Will and Grace try to get pregnant,

Nurse Sheila is there to collect the samples. She also speaks at Jack's graduation from nursing school. Nurse Sheila pops up again in the final season in Grace's Lamaze class. Since they last saw her, she was fired from the fertility clinic, and has since knocked herself up with a sample of stolen Irish sperm. "I wanna be able to drink with my kid," she explains. Vince, Will's boyfriend, gets stuck as her Lamaze coach.

Julie, played by Rosanna Arquette

Julie is Grace's neighbor once Grace moves into Leo's building in Brooklyn. Julie, a masseuse, gives Grace a massage and gets a little too grabby. Julie's husband is an actor best known for his work as Aladdin in the mall.

Zandra Zoggin, played by Eileen Brennan

QUOTE

"And do you know why they're coming with me, Zandra? Because I touched people in this class today. And when no one was looking, I touched myself a little bit, too."

—Jack McFarland

Zandra is Jack's tough-as-nails acting teacher with whom he studies for roughly five years. Eventually Jack's lack of talent prompts Zandra to kick him out of class. The other students follow Jack and he creates his own school of acting: the McFarland Method. Zandra spends her final days living in the Actors' Retirement Village taking tubs with *The Facts of Life*'s Charlotte Rae.

The Colleagues

Harlin Polk, played by Gary Grubbs

Harlin Polk, a rich Texan, is introduced in "The Pilot" as one of Will's most prominent clients. Harlin is a frank, no-nonsense sort. When Will invites him up to the apartment, Harlin witnesses an icy conversation between him and Grace and comments: "Will, are you sure you're gay? 'Cause this felt exactly like a night between me and the Mrs." Harlin hires Grace to design his new apartment in Season 1, but when Grace caters more to Harlin's rancher taste than Will's Chelsea preferences, Will and Grace duke it out. Harlin sticks around for the rest of Season 1, but in Season 2 he fires Will.

Q FACT

Eileen Brennan was nominated for an Emmy for Outstanding Guest Actress in a Comedy Series in 2004 for her portrayal of Zandra.

Will, who had dumped all his other clients to devote his time exclusively to the wealthy Harlin, is suddenly left with no practice.

Mr. Stein, played by Gene Wilder

Mr. Stein, the other half of Will's firm, Doucette and Stein, returns in Season 5 to whip the company into shape. He comes across as a shouting, swaggering tyrant of a boss, but when Will runs into Stein crouching on a toilet in panic, Stein's brutish façade falls apart. For the last three years, Stein had not been at the London office, as everyone believed, but was a resident at a loony bin. Will helps Stein cover up his insanity and Stein repays Will with lavish, career-boosting favors. Eventually, Will's co-workers grow bitter and Will realizes Stein's dependence on him is unhealthy. Will talks Stein into being his old self again—a shark, a barracuda—and Stein is momentarily back to fighting shape. Stein later appears in Season 5 when he joins Will and Karen in drowning their sorrows over their wrecked love lives. Karen and Stein make out, too!

Q FACT

Gene Wilder won an Emmy Award for Outstanding Guest Actor in 2003 for his portrayal of Mr. Stein, Will's never before seen, unhinged boss.

Margot, played by Lily Tomlin

Margot, the tactless new senior partner at Doucette and Stein, first appears in Season 7. Will is up for partner and Margot invites Will along with the other two candidates to a dinner party at her house. The evening is meant to be a competition, although Margot had secretly decided Will would be promoted all along. Margot also invites Grace under the pretense of setting her up on a blind date—the man turns out to be Margot's elderly and spank-happy husband, Leonard (Buck Henry). Later in Season 8, after Will has quit the firm to do more "noble" work for the Coalition for Justice, Margot lures him back and hires Grace to redecorate the law firm.

Dorleen, played by Parker Posey

QUOTE

"It's dark. It's glam. It's sad. It's Christmas."

—Dorleen

When Jack is fired from Banana Republic, he gets a job as a "salesgirl" at Barneys under the supervision of floor manager Dorleen. Dorleen is a dictator who takes her job at Barneys New York very seriously. When Dorleen gets a load of the man candy that is Will Truman, she decides to give Jack a requested Friday night off in exchange for a date with Will. Jack sends an un-suspecting Will to Dorleen first under the pretense of delivering flowers, and then as a potential model for Barney's. Later, when Dorleen strips for Will, the truth comes out. Dorleen demotes Jack to Hand Creams. Months later, out of desperation, Dorleen allows Jack to design one of the store windows for the holidays. Grace bails Jack out at the last minute, creating an amazing display that even the hard-to-please Dorleen approves.

One-Timers

Neil, played by Dan Bucatinsky, Episode 221, "The Hospital Show"

Neil is Will's mother's dentist's bridge partner's son. Neil thinks he's God's gift to gay men. "If that's true, then God shops at the Newark airport," snarks Will. As a favor to his mother, Will agrees to go on a date with Neil, who greets Will with a "ready to get Neiled?" Will ditches him when Stan has a heart attack, but Neil follows Will to the hospital and continues the pursuit.

Helena Barnes, played by Joan Collins, Episode 220, "My Best Friend's Tush"

Helena Barnes is an "international design goddess," ac-cording to Grace. Helena secretly enjoys Taco Time (a guilty pleasure for the ladies in her circle), where she sucks down tacos with her little dog, Paxil, by her side and in her purse. At Taco Time Karen uses her alias Anastasia Beaverhousen and Helena uses the name Endora.

Bill, played by Neil Patrick Harris, Episode 222, "Girls, Interrupted"

Bill is the leader of the local "Welcome Back Home" chapter. When Bill meets Jack at a club he gives him a flyer for his group, which Jack reads as "Welcome Back Homo." Karen explains the group's purpose (turning gay people straight) and Jack makes Karen go with him to the meeting so that Jack can "shine the mirror of truth upon them." And make out with Bill. At the meeting, Jack tries to release Bill's "inner homo" by inviting Bill to shower with him. Bill is offended and addresses the group to make certain that everyone is there for the right reasons: "We are here to lead normal, heterosexual lives. Man and woman are meant to be together. So anyone here who has a misguided notion that Welcome Back Home is some kind of a—a gay pickup joint, you can just leave right now." The room quickly empties. Bill decides to shower with Jack as long as it's "a heterosexual soap-down."

Gillian, played by Natasha Lyonne, Episode 303, "Girl Trouble"

Gillian, a design student at Cooper Union, has a brief stint as an intern at Grace Adler Designs. When Gillian arrives she wants to be like Grace . . . until she meets Karen. Gillian goes on long shopping sprees and takes to calling everyone "Honey."

Psychic Sue, played by Camryn Manheim, Episode 312, "Gypsies, Tramps, and Weed"

Psychic Sue is a dead-on fortune-teller who gives Will a disturbing prediction: He will spend the rest of his life with a man named . . . Jack.

Sister Louise, played by Ellen DeGeneres, Episode 315, "My Uncle the Car"

Sister Louise is the proud owner of Uncle Jerry's car, the lemon Grace's uncle left her when he passed away. Sister Louise buys the car on the cheap for her side business, a cheesecake delivery company called "What a Friend We Have in Cheesecake." When Grace decides she wants the car back, Sister Louise offers her an unreasonably high asking price. Will convinces Louise to give up the car, but in exchange Will and Grace help out with the cheesecake deliveries.

Kevin Wolchek, played by Adam Goldberg, Episode 402, "Past and Presents"

Back in elementary school, Kevin used to dump Will in the cafeteria garbage if Will didn't do the bully's homework. When Kevin joins Doucette & Stein, Kevin tries to repeat the pattern, intimidating Will into doing his work.

Owen, played by Matt Damon, Episode 419, "A Chorus Lie"

Owen, a "howdy-doody-looking motherfella," according to Jack, is Jack's competition for the last spot in the Gay Men's Chorus, which is set to tour Europe later in the year. Owen is a straight man who pretends to be gay so he can participate in the chorus. Jack gets wise to Owen's faux gay routine, and sets out to "in" him using Grace and her feminine wiles. The plan works and Owen is forced to reveal to the chorus his true sexual

QUOTE

"There's something very southern about Matt Damon. He's like 'Yes, Ma'am. No, Sir.' He's 'please.' He's 'thank you.' He's so beautifully reared. And he's a hugger. He just wanted to hug everybody. He's like this overgrown puppy dog and physically the warmest human being. He gave me this big hug and I just thought, 'Wow. Here we are. Me and Matt Damon.'"

—Leslie Jordan ("Beverly Leslie")

orientation. Owen explains to the others that, for him, singing choral music is like "being gently chucked under the chin by God" and sadly "there's no room for a straight man in that world." The chorus, which has a "tolerance" policy, chooses Owen over Jack.

Detective Gavin Hatch, played by Michael Douglas, Episode 421, "Fagel Attraction"

When Will's laptop is stolen at a coffee shop, Detective Hatch uses the crime as an excuse to get closer to Will. He invites Will to go on an "undercover" sting operation that grows increasingly elaborate and difficult to maintain. The two find themselves staking out a gay bar and end up dancing to Missy Elliot's "Get Ur Freak On." Still, the jig isn't up until Will runs into Jack, who outs the detective as "Freaky Teeth Guy" from his therapy group. Will effectively ends his mission with the detective by filling his teeth with obnoxious spinach dip.

Fannie Lieber, played by Glenn Close, Episode 424, "Hocus Focus"

At an HRC auction, Will wins a photo session with Fannie and invites Grace to be in the pictures with

Q FACT

Michael Douglas was nominated for an Outstanding Guest Actor Emmy in 2002 for his role as the lovelorn gay detective Gavin Hatch.

him. Using Red Bull to fill the void of narcotics, Fannie is a whirling dervish of a lenswoman, forcing Will and Grace into bizarre poses. Unhappy with the photos, Will and Grace repeatedly return to Fannie to take another set. Frustrated, Fannie chastises them for obsessing over their appearance in a picture. She urges them to do "something. Have a baby. I don't know. I don't care. Just get out of my life." Although said in jest, Fannie's words strike a chord with Will and Grace, and in the following episode they embark down the baby path.

Milo, played by Andy Garcia, Episode 512, "Field of Queens"

Milo, a suave, playboy restaurant owner, goes on a date with Karen, tells her he'll call, and then doesn't! Grace confronts Milo and he explains that he wasn't interested in Karen because she's too old for him, even though they're the same age. Then he tries to kiss Grace. Disgusted, Grace tells him he'll end up alone, though the woman who suddenly pops up and kisses him kills that theory.

Q FACT

Glenn Close was nominated for an Emmy for Outstanding Guest Actor in 2002 for her portrayal of newly sober, freaky celebrity photog Fannie Lieber.

Sissy, played by Demi Moore, Episode 517, "Women and Children First"

Sissy was Jack's fun babysitter, the one who let him watch *Auntie Mame* over and over again when he was nine years old. Since babysitting for Jack, Sissy got herself a Eurail Pass and babysat her way through Europe. When Jack runs into her in the present day, Sissy picks up right where she left off and resumes as Jack's babysitter, making sure he gets enough sleep and eats well. Jack eventually fires her when he learns Sissy's jacked up her rates to $40 an hour.

Liz, played by Madonna, Episode 521, "Dolls and Dolls"

Madonna's prime-time television debut was on April 24, 2003, as Karen's new fussbudget roommate, Liz. For fun, Karen wants to live as a commoner and answers a roommate ad posted by "Non-Smoker Liz" at a Laundromat. Liz, an office manager for a company that produces eighties and nineties compilations, runs a tight ship in her apartment—there's a chore wheel and strict rules about going after the same guy. At first Karen finds Liz and her quirks (she loves saying "cut to") fascinating, but after they go for the same guy Liz wants Karen out. Since Karen owns Liz's building, Karen gets to evict Liz instead.

Jason Towne, aka JT, played by Macaulay Culkin, Episode 522, "May Divorce Be with You"

JT is Karen's youthful, seemingly incompetent lawyer. Even though Will represents Stan, he feels sorry for

QUOTE

"Between scenes the band played one of Madonna's songs—I think it was 'Lucky Star'—while we were setting up. She was standing by herself readying to enter the apartment scene and I saw her full-on dancing to her own song in the dark waiting for her cue. I thought 'I'm the only person witnessing this surreal moment.'"

—Jon Kinnally, Writer and Executive Producer

Karen's inept whippersnapper attorney. Will feeds JT some helpful information only to find out JT's been playing him like "pong." In reality, JT is a shark who scored a killer settlement for Debbie Harry, which she thanked him for by "rocking his world" in the back of his Mercedes. After he reveals his scheme to Karen, he advises her to get a bikini wax because he likes "a clean workspace."

Dr. Danielle Morty, played by Nicollette Sheridan, Episode 524, "24"

Dr. Morty is the hot doctor Leo will be serving with in Guatemela for Doctors Without Borders. When Dr. Morty, in all her blondeness, first meets the fab four, Grace tries to remain calm. As soon as the doc leaves the room, Jack screams: "Aren't you dying?! Your husband is going to Guatemala with *that!* I would *die!*" Things get worse when Grace discovers a letter Dr. Morty slipped into Leo's bag describing her lust for Grace's husband. Leo convinces Grace that he has no interest in Dr. Morty.

Tom, played by Dylan McDermott, Episode 605, "Heart Like a Wheelchair"

Tom is a gorgeous Mama's boy Will meets in the park while both men take their wheelchair-bound mothers for walks. Tom is turned off by men who don't love their mothers, so naturally Will lays it on thick. When Marilyn's injury heals enough for her to not need the wheelchair anymore, Will insists she stay in it so that he can have an excuse to flirt with Tom in the park. Marilyn goes along with it for the sake of her son. When Will and Tom finally get some alone time, Ruth, Tom's decrepit mother, injures herself making Jiffy Pop. Tom blames Will and their romance quickly fizzles out.

Q FACT

Dr. Hershberg's sister, and disturbing crush, is none other than Nurse Sheila (Laura Kightlinger), last seen handling Will's sperm in Season 5.

Dr. Isaac Hershberg, played by Jack Black, Episode 606, "Nice in White Satin"

Will accompanies Karen to an appointment with the wacky Dr. Hershberg, who makes jokes about cups of pee resembling lemonade. Also disconcerting, Dr. Hershberg has no diplomas on his wall.

Cheryl, aka "Copacafana 82," played by Sarah Gilbert, Episode 611, "Fanilow"

Will meets Cheryl on the line for a "Very Barry Christmas" starring Barry Manilow, but Will and Cheryl have actually met before in a chat room where Will goes by the name No. One Fanilow (it looks like "no one fanilow").

Alan Mills, played by Hal Linden, Episode 612, "A Gay/December Romance"

Alan, a rich plastic surgeon, showers Will with presents after they meet at a gallery. When Will's friends point out that he has a sugar daddy, Will decides to confront Alan about his intentions. Alan is offended by Will's insinuation. However, after that conversation, Alan dumps Will and begins throwing presents at a new "boy toy."

QUOTE

"Even though I live alone, nobody likes me at work, and I follow a 57-year-old pop singer around the country, this is boring, so . . . Could you just talk to the person on the other side of you?"

—Cheryl, to Grace after listening to Grace's marriage woes

Ann, played by Tracey Ullman, Episode 614, "Looking for Mr. Good Enough"

Ann, a chef with a dishwasher-safe prosthetic hand, teaches a cooking class that Will, Larry, Joe, Jack, and his boyfriend Stuart attend. Surrounded by cooking couples, Will feels especially lonely. Sympathetic, Ann secretly hires Adam, a hunky prostitute, to hit on Will. As she says, "When my husband died, it wasn't soup that comforted me. It was Adam."

Monet, played by Chloe Sevigny, Episode 617, "East Side Story"

Monet is one half of the "Flipping Dykes," also known as D & M properties, New York's power lesbian realtors.

Monet's better half (and dominating partner) is Deirdre, played by Edie Falco. Deirdre forces interior designer and reluctant lesbian Monet to stay out of the sun and starve herself to maintain the pale and bony look Deirdre likes. Although Monet is hooked up with Deirdre, her lusty advances toward Will reveal she may not be committed to playing on Deirdre's team.

Deirdre, played by Edie Falco, Episode 617, "East Side Story"

Deirdre is the realty expert and dominating personality of D & M properties, aka the "Flipping Dykes." Deirdre hatches a plan to steal Grace from Will, replacing Monet as her designer. The plan nearly works because Deirdre tells Grace she's "pretty." Ultimately all partnerships remain intact, and Will and Grace agree not to pursue properties in the Flipping Dyke territory of the East Side.

Nadine, played by Kristin Davis, Episode 707, "Will & Grace & Vince & Nadine"

QUOTE

"You're obnoxious and over-bearing and your food is too pretentious. I mean, even your chicken had a Swiss chard vest. And you're too groomed. If your eyebrows were tweezed any more, you'd be Nicole Kidman! I can't even stand to look at you for one more second!"

—Nadine on Will

Nadine is Vince's "Grace," but the two sets of best friends couldn't be more different. Nadine and Vince are nice to each other, whereas Will and Grace constantly bicker. Grace tries to coax Nadine into revealing one thing she can't stand about Vince and when she does it's a doozy: She hates Will. Will worries that "if the hag hates you, the fag don't date you!" so Grace tries to make things right with Nadine. While shopping, Grace tells Nadine she knows what's going on: Nadine wants Vince all for herself. Grace understands because she was Nadine years ago, but Vince is gay and they will never be together. Grace convinces Nadine to move on, and she joyously declares she won't give herself "little cuts" on her leg that day.

Peter Bovington, played by Victor Garber, Episode 709, "Saving Grace, Again" (Part 2)

Peter Bovington was a camp icon in the seventies known best for his Sinfully Delicious Cocoa Devil commercials in which he'd say, "It's sinfully delicious." When Jack runs into Peter working at a hotel, Jack thinks fate has brought him the perfect spokesperson for Out TV. Unfortunately, Peter, who did three years at Williamstown, two seasons at the Guthrie, and spent a winter at the Old Vic, wants to be a serious actor and distance himself from his devilish catchphrase. When Jack tells him his line will be "Watch Out TV. It's sinfully delicious," Peter throws a hissy and walks out.

Ro, played by Jamie-Lynn DiScala, Episode 710, "Queens for a Day"

Ro is Vince's closeted lesbian sister. Vince brings Will to his family's home in Queens for Thanksgiving. Over the course of the day, Ro outs herself to Jack and later Will outs Ro to her family at the dinner table. Ro has a crush on Renée Zellweger.

Leonard, played by Buck Henry, Episode 713, "Partners"

Will's boss, Margot, invites Grace to attend her dinner party using a blind setup as bait. The date turns out to be Leonard, Margot's husband, who wants to be spanked.

Aaron, played by Luke Perry, Episode 716, "The Birds and the Bees"

Aaron is a "Hot Gay Nerd" who likes bird-watching. Aaron is shy, and when Jack asks him out he "flits" away. In an effort to make the two men lovebirds, Karen steals Aaron's bird and has him come up to her penthouse. Unfortunately she accidentally kills the bird by giving it gin. Karen makes everything okay when she gives Aaron $78,000 and $100 in iTunes.

Edward, aka "Pastry Chef," played by Stewart Townsend, Episode 717, "The Fabulous Baker Boy"

Edward is a "pansexual" pastry chef. When Will goes over Karen's budget, he decides she can afford to lose Pastry Chef. But when Will meets the dashing Edward, Will forgets about firing him and instead Edward "sexes" him. Later, Karen, curious as to why Will suddenly changed his mind, meets Edward and he sexes her, too. Will is upset, thinking Edward and he were going to start seeing each other or at the very least go away for the weekend. Then it is revealed that Edward is also sexing Rosie, and Will's fantasy comes to an end.

Dr. Georgia, played by Sharon Stone, Episode 719, "The Blonde Leading the Blind"

According to Will, his shrink Dr. Georgia is "tough but good." An example of Dr. Georgia's therapy: She makes Will write a letter to his younger self apologizing for what he's become. Will's personal growth is stymied when Grace sees the good doctor and becomes the shrink's case study for a new book. Will is jealous, and the two compete to be case studies, each trying to outcrazy the other one.

Randall Finn, played by Seth Green, Episode 722, "Friends with Benefits"

Randall is a former child star and current telemarketer when he agrees to host Jack's new talk show for Out TV. Randall is a diva from the beginning, treating the "crew" (just Jack) poorly, making unruly demands, and showing up late for a taped segment. Randall provokes Jack into a fistfight, which Jack wins with a single slap. Randall quits in a huff.

Dale, played by Andy Richter, Episode 803, "The Old Man and the Sea"

Dale is Malcolm Widmark's sad sack friend who lives in Staten Island on top of a landfill. Malcolm and Karen drag Grace on a double date with them and Dale. Dale tortures Grace with his poetry, but manages to woo her when he prepares chicken *with* skin and plays show tunes on the piano. But when Grace starts singing using her perfect ear-bleeding pitch, Dale rescinds his woo and tries to get her to leave.

The Q Guide to Will & Grace

Amber-Louise, played by Britney Spears, Episode 818, "Buy Buy Baby"

On the surface, Amber-Louise is a conservative, acid-tongued southern belle. But the real Amber-Louise is a lesbian named Peg who enjoys "leather play, butch black girls, skunkin', pullin' the blinds, and poodle-ballin'." When Out TV is bought by Nimbus Television Networks (owned by Digicity Global Worldwide, a division of the Department of Homeland Security), *Jack Talk* gets a makeover in the form of Amber-Louise's Bible Belt homecoming queen, who supports torture and hates gays. At first Jack refuses to work with Amber-Louise, but she pulls him aside and confesses that she's really the other kind of bush lover. She's just compromising so she can live the dream of earning $165 a week and being on television. Jack tries to go with the new right-wing flow of *Jack Talk,* but when he has to pretend *Star Trek*'s George Takei, a celebrated "prancing, giggling queen," is a "ladies' man" and "pro-life activist," Jack can't take it anymore. Later he begs Amber-Louise for his job back but she refuses.

The Stars As Themselves

Al Roker, Episode 214, "Acting Out"

When Will and Jack tune in to watch the first prime-time network kiss by two gay men on fictional sitcom *Along Came You*, they are deeply disappointed. Instead of a kiss between "flamers" they get a screenshot of a fireplace. Outraged, Jack and Will go down to NBC studios and "stick it to the man." After being brushed off by a network honcho, they find themselves in the throng of *Today Show* fans mugging for face time with Al Roker. Jack demands to know how long he's going to have to wait to see a network air a kiss between two men. With the *Today Show* cameras rolling, Will decides "not as long as you'd think" and plants one on Jack.

Sandra Bernhard, Episode 304, "Swimming Pools . . . Movie Stars," and Episode 415, "Someone Old, Someplace New"

In "Swimming Pools . . . Movie Stars," Sandra's apartment is listed in the real estate section, which puts her on Will and Grace's radar. As big Sandra fans, it is their duty to see her place, even though they have no interest in buying it. But when Sandra meets them, she decides she wants to sell her place to the "happening gay guy and the vivacious redhead." Under the pretense of buying her apartment, Will and Grace briefly pal around with Sandra. Grace even scores an invite to join Sandra on stage at the Bottom Line. Eventually they confess to Sandra that they really just want to be her friends, not her apartment's new owners. Sandra lets loose a flurry of strong language that's censored by the sounds of a nearby blender. Sandra is disgusted that Will and Grace are just another pair of "Looky-losers" who just want to see a celeb in her "natural habitat." Sandra reappears briefly in Season 4 when Will and Grace decide they're ready for a bigger place. They accidentally go to an open house at Sandra's and she picks up where she left off, screaming curses censored by convenient drill noises.

Cher, Episode 312, "Gypsies, Tramps, and Weed," and Episode 426/427, "A.I. Artificial Insemination Part I & II"

In Season 3's "Gypsies, Tramps, and Weed," Jack grows obsessed with his new Cher doll. But when he encounters his idol in the flesh, he mistakes Cher for a drag queen. After Cher pulls a *Moonstruck*, slapping Jack and telling him to "snap out of it!" Jack realizes his mistake and faints. In Season 4 Jack's been toiling away in retail, convinced he belongs there until Cher appears to him in a dream. As a God-like entity she tells Jack to follow his bliss and return to showbiz.

Kevin Bacon, Episode 501, "Bacon and Eggs," and Episode 823, "The Finale"

QUOTE

"When the stalkers leave, it's the first sign that your career is slipping."

—Kevin Bacon

In his first appearance Kevin Bacon portrays Kevin Bacon as an insecure, narcissistic actor, clinging to fame. Jack takes his stalking of Kevin Bacon to the next level, and accidentally gets swept up in a pool of applicants for Kevin's new personal assistant. Jack is hired and charged with finding out the identity of Kevin's stalker. To cover up his own spying, Jack leads Kevin to believe that Will is the peeper. Kevin takes Will back to his house to confront him and then is deeply disappointed when Will has no interest in stalking him. Kevin tries to tempt Will into stalking him, even persuading Will to join him in the legendary *Footloose* dance. Jack walks in on them and declares himself the real stalker. Kevin apologizes to Jack for not realizing, and the three continue the routine. Kevin is last seen in Grace's dream sequence in "The Finale," where she imagines a future where Jack and Kevin are married, Jack having "stalked him all the way to the altar."

Katie Couric, Episode 508, "Marry Me a Little/Marry Me a Little More"

In Central Park, Grace and Leo run into Katie Couric conducting a mass wedding for a segment on the *Today* show. Katie suggests Leo and Grace join in the wedding, since they seem like a happy couple.

Sir Elton John, Episode 510,
"The Honeymoon's Over"

QUOTE

"Don't dismiss things you know nothing about. And don't walk in ten-inch heels—it's hell on the ankles."

—Sir Elton John, Don of the Gay Mafia

Jack fears the gay mafia has put a "hit" out on him for kicking a student out of his acting class. Will dismisses Jack's fears about the existence of a gay mafia. Later, at a restaurant, Will learns he's wrong when he meets the Don himself, Sir Elton John. Before leaving, Sir Elton gets two dollars from Will for the coat-check girl.

Deborah Harry, Episode 524, "24"

Debbie Harry attends Stan's wake. In the episode, we learn that when someone walks in on her in the bathroom she just goes right on peeing. Also her friendship with Karen fell apart when Debbie ran out of weed.

James Earl Jones, Episode 604, "Me and Mr. Jones"

Jack lands a one-line role in *The Iceman Cometh* alongside acting legend James Earl Jones. Surprisingly, their director feels that Jack brings more to his role than James. At first James is angry, saying he doesn't have to put up with that kind of treatment because he has "Darth Vader money." But after Karen gets in a few gibes, James feels insecure and worries he's a fraud. When he learns that Jack is a teacher, he enrolls in his class to glean what he can from the McFarland Method. In class, Jack tries to get James to speak in a higher-pitched voice, to "lose the James Earl Jones, and find the James Girl Jones." He gives James a scene from *Sex and the City* where he plays Carrie. James is forced to repeat "Jimmy Choos" in a falsetto voice over and over again. Jack's class helps James rediscover acting basics as he realizes that Jack knows nothing about acting. After the opening night performance, James changes into Juicy Couture sweats

QUOTE

"A favorite guest star moment was when Sean gives James Earl Jones a scene from *Sex and the City*. Jack tells him to say 'Jimmy Choos' over and over in an increasingly higher voice."

—Tracy Poust, Writer and Executive Producer

and meets up with Karen in front of Sardi's so she can ride on his shoulders for a few minutes.

Candice "Candy" Bergen, Episode 607, "Strangers with Candice"

Candice Bergen is Karen's nemesis/former makeout buddy. The two women delight in playing vicious pranks on each other, usually capped off by a "gotcha!"

Barry Manilow, Episode 611, "Fanilow"

Will loves Barry Manilow so much he's willing to go on a date with a horrible roadie just to meet him. When Will finally meets his idol, they do a duet of "American Bandstand."

Bebe Neuwirth, Episode 619, "No Sex 'n' the City"

At a coffee shop, Jack and Karen lament the end of *Sex and the City*, when they spot Bebe Neuwirth, known best for her role as icy Lilith on *Frasier* and *Cheers*. Starstruck, they fawn all over her and Jack tells her she has the body of "fourteen-year-old Korean gymnast." At first Bebe is put off by Karen and Jack refusing to call her by any other name but Lilith. However, she eventually admits she's upset about *Frasier* ending, and that when it comes to Lilith, she wants "to play that bitch forever."

Jennifer Lopez, Episodes 623/624, "I Do" and "Oh No, You Di-in't," and Episode 701, "FYI: I Hurt Too"

Karen runs into Jennifer Lopez in the bathroom at Caesars Palace on the eve of her wedding to Lyle Finster. Jennifer and Karen go way back, having first met through Rosario when J-Lo and Karen's future maid took tap together in the Bronx. Doing a fun parody of her multibranded self, Jennifer tells Karen she's been taking it easy these days, only shooting a movie in L.A, working on a new line of track suits, studying for her real estate license, opening a restaurant, mixing a new CD, and finishing a novel. Despite Jennifer's busy schedule, Karen still hits her up for a performance at her wedding.

Karen introduces Jennifer as "Jen Pez" to her guests and Jennifer takes the stage. Suddenly, one of her backup dancers slips on a discarded shrimp tail and injures himself. Both Beverly Leslie and Jack offer to step in, but Jennifer chooses Jack. She performs "Waiting for Tonight," ending the song with Jack posing underneath her leg. Jennifer eventually gives Jack to Janet Jackson.

QUOTE

"Jennifer Lopez was very sweet and very game."

—Jon Kinnally, Writer and Executive Producer, on Working with J-Lo

"She was so accessible. She was so nervous. She said, 'I haven't done a lot of comedy,' and then she was wildly funny. They were only dating at the time, but Marc Anthony was there. When you first see him you think he's in her shadow. She's so beautiful, so he's just not as attractive as she is. But all of a sudden, he came over and took my hands and looked in my eyes and said, 'What a gift. To be able to make people laugh. You must just thank God every day for that. What a wonderful gift.' And I just thought, 'I'm so in love with Jennifer Lopez's boyfriend! I just fell head over heels for Jennifer Lopez's boyfriend!' He was such a dear dear kid."

—Leslie Jordan ("Beverly Leslie"),
on working with J-Lo

Janet Jackson, Episode 702, "Back Up, Dancer"

Jack auditions to be one of Janet's backup dancers. At rehearsal she makes an entrance in a cloud of smoke, which "costs a little extra," but she makes up for it by having the dancers pay for their own costumes. Janet ends up cutting Jack from the squad.

Rip Taylor, Episode 709, "Saving Grace, Again" (Part 2)

Rip Taylor is all set to be the new face of Out TV until Jack shows up with another gay icon, the Sinfully Delicious Cocoa Devil (Victor Garber). Rip is fired on the spot and, even though he's upset, he can't resist tossing up confetti. One of the Out TV staff is kind enough to drive him to the bus stop.

Patti LuPone, Episode 714, "Bully Woolley"

Patti LuPone is one of Jack's favorite divas, but when he runs into her at Barney's Café, he forces himself to avoid her because he promised Will he would give him his undivided attention. Jack wants to cut Patti's hair and make a wig like the one he assembled from the cast of the *Golden Girls*. Will is touched that Jack spurns a Broadway legend for him, but insists that Jack commence with the scalping. At the end of the episode, Patti performs "Don't Cry for Me Argentina" from *Evita*, the musical for which she won a Tony.

Matt Lauer, Episode 811, "Bathroom Humor"

Matt Lauer appears in *Will & Grace*'s second live episode. He's a guest at Karen's exclusive party at the Walker penthouse. The entire episode takes place with the main cast in a bathroom. Matt pops in twice, trying to "tinkle," and in the episode's final moments he can hold it in no longer. It is revealed he sits down when he pees.

Darryl Hall and John Oates, Episode 815, "The Definition of Marriage"

Karen hires Hall and Oates to play at the green card wedding of Grace and Will's boyfriend, James. When

LESLIE JORDAN ON MEETING MATT LAUER

When I heard that Matt Lauer was coming, I just thought I was going to faint. Seldom are we mortals allowed to be in the presence of such a God-like creature. He was so nice. The first thing you notice is he's nine feet tall and skinny skinny skinny. I think he's better looking than anything Hollywood ever put out. He's not classically handsome. He's just got it. Whatever it is. And he would try to talk to me and I would just giggle like a shy Japanese girl behind my hand fan. I thought, "He probably thinks I'm retarded."

He was involved with the live episode "Bathroom Humor." Every once in a while the writers would toss in something, and we would just look at each other and think, "We can't say that!" So the joke was I come into the bathroom and then I run out, and it's the middle of a party. Will forgets he doesn't have his pants

they arrive they explain that they are now "Oates and Hall"—they switch every twenty-five years. At the ceremony, they serve not only as hired musicians but also may have to clean dirty dishes, and apparently Oates is expected to do caricatures for a dollar.

on and storms out, and he was supposed to sheepishly say, "In case anyone's interested, Beverly Leslie comes up to my penis." And then Debra had a line, "Oh, you just teabagged a dwarf." Sure enough, immediately we heard from the censors: "Teabag can be used as a noun. Teabag cannot be used as a verb." Well, Matt leans in to me and says, "Is that term that popular?" And I thought he didn't know what it meant. So without thinking I said, "Oh you know, it's when you take your balls and put them in someone else's mouth . . ." and he looks at me and says, "I know what it means!" I was just mortified. I wanted the floor to open up and swallow me.

The teabag joke was replaced with a joke where Matt Lauer reveals he sits down when he pees. I thought, "Well, that's a good sport." I also thought, "Oh Lord, I may be famous one day and they'll ask me to do the *Today* show and Matt Lauer will say, "'Gosh no, he might talk about his gonads in somebody's mouth!'"

—Leslie Jordan ("Beverly Leslie")

Josh Lucas, Episode 822, "Whatever Happened to Baby Gin?"

Jack briefly befriends Josh Lucas and learns that the actor's real voice is a squeaky chirp. Apparently, "all the top leading men are dubbed," according to the star.

CHAPTER SEVEN

Episode Summaries

Season 1

"The Pilot"
Episode #101, Original Air Date 9/21/1998
Written by David Kohan and Max Mutchnick
Directed by James Burrows
After Will plants seeds of doubt in Grace's head,
    she leaves fiancé Danny at the altar.

"A New Lease on Life"
Episode #102, Original Air Date 9/28/1998
Written by David Kohan and Max Mutchnick
Directed by James Burrows
Grace wants to move in with Will but he's against the
    idea. But once Grace takes an apartment in Brooklyn,
    Will realizes he wants her as a roomie after all.

"Head Case"
Episode #103, Original Air Date 10/5/1998
Written by David Kohan & Max Mutchnick
Directed by James Burrows
New roommates Grace and Will run into problems

when they decide to combine their two bathrooms into one gigantic bathroom.

"Where There's a Will, There's No Way"
Episode #104, Original Air Date 11/16/1998
Written by Jhoni Marchinko
Directed by James Burrows
Grace puts a moratorium on her "us-ness" with Will so that she can have room in her life to date. Meanwhile, Jack finds himself in trouble with the IRS for never having paid his taxes. Will pays off Jack's debt.

"Will on Ice"
Episode #105, Original Air Date 1/12/1999
Written by Michael Patrick King
Directed by James Burrows
Will's birthday plans are derailed when Jack gets four tickets to "Champions on Ice" at Madison Square Garden.

"William, Tell"
Episode #106, Original Air Date 11/9/1998
Written by William Lucas Walker
Directed by James Burrows
Jack subs for Karen as Grace's assistant for the week. They swap "Will Secrets" and come to the conclusion that Will is currently keeping a doozy. Grace becomes obsessed with finding out Will's secret. Later she admits that she's always afraid Will will deliver another life-altering secret to her just as he did when he came out years ago.

"Boo! Humbug!"
Episode #107, Original Air Date 10/7/1998
Written by Jon Kinnally & Tracy Poust
Directed by James Burrows
Just as Will and Grace are about to venture out for their
    wild "adult" Halloween, Harlin drops his kids off for
    impromptu babysitting. Meanwhile, Karen is wor-
    shiped by drag queens.

"The Truth About Will and Dogs"
Episode #108, Original Air Date 12/15/1998
Written by David Kohan & Max Mutchnick
Directed by James Burrows
Lonely Hearts Will and Grace get a puppy but soon
    realize they are channeling all their love and affection
    into the pooch instead of moving on to find new
    significant others.

"Grace Replaced"
Episode #109, Original Air Date 4/8/1999
Written by Katie Palmer
Directed by James Burrows
When things heat up at Grace's work, Will feels ne-
    glected. New eccentric neighbor Val (Molly Shannon)
    seems the perfect replacement. But Grace doesn't like
    being replaced and Val proves herself a lunatic. Val is
    quickly booted from Will and Grace's life.

"Secrets and Lays"
Episode #110, Original Air Date 3/23/1999
Written by Dava Savel
Directed by James Burrows

To keep Will's mind off what would have been his
anniversary with Michael, Grace, Jack, and Karen
take him to Karen's Vermont cabin.

"Between a Rock and Harlin's Place"
Episode #111, Original Air Date 10/12/1998
Written by David Kohan & Max Mutchnick
Directed by James Burrows
When Harlin hires Grace to redecorate his new apart-
ment in New York, Will causes problems when he
openly critiques Grace's "cowboy"-chic choices.

"The Buying Game"
Episode #112, Original Air Date 11/30/1998
Written by Dava Saval
Directed by James Burrows
Will helps Grace buy her office space but his strategy
involves painting Grace as a naïve sap. Grace
proves her business acumen when she manages
to get the desperate landlord to sell to her at a
reduced price.

"My Fair Maid-y"
Episode #113, Original Air Date 2/2/1999
Written by Adam Barr
Directed by James Burrows
Grace suffers designer's block so Will surprises Grace
by hiring a maid, April (Wendy Jo Sperber), to help
organize her work space. April becomes a muse for
Grace and soon Grace feels she cannot design with-
out April's help.

"Will Works Out"
Episode #114, Original Air Date 5/6/1999
Written by Michael Patrick King and Jon Kinnally &
    Tracy Poust
Directed by James Burrows
Jack joins Will and Grace's gym, where many of Will's
    clients also work out. Will worries Jack will embar-
    rass him in front of his clients, lamenting to Grace,
    "sometimes Jack is such a fag." Jack overhears him
    and tries to act like a straight meathead. Will
    realizes he's actually envious of Jack's comfort with
    himself.

"The Big Vent"
Episode #115, Original Air Date 1/5/1999
Story by Jon Kinnally & Tracy Poust, Teleplay by Jhoni
    Marchinko
Directed by James Burrows
Will and Grace become obsessed with their neighbors'
    drama, which they hear courtesy of a heating vent.

"Big Brother Is Coming, Part I"
Episode #116, Original Air Date 2/16/1999
Written by David Kohan & Max Mutchnick
Directed by James Burrows
Grace runs into Will's estranged brother Sam and
    attempts to reunite the brothers. After much resis-
    tance Will and Sam finally make amends. But when
    Will rushes out to comfort Jack over turning 30 (not
    29, as he had thought), Sam and Grace share a pas-
    sionate kiss.

"Big Brother Is Coming, Part II"
Episode #117, Original Air Date 2/23/1999
Written by David Kohan & Max Mutchnick
Directed by James Burrows
Grace and Sam sleep together but decide to keep their
    affair a secret from Will. When Will finds out, he is
    angry but soon realizes that he needs to accept Grace
    and Sam's relationship. Grace, sensing the problems
    dating Sam would cause, breaks it off with him.

"The Unsinkable Mommy Adler"
Episode #118, Original Air Date 2/9/1999
Written by Alex Herschleg
Directed by James Burrows
Grace's mother, Bobbi Adler (Debbie Reynolds), sweeps
    into town and causes quite a stir by suggesting Grace
    should marry Will. When Will says that even if he
    were straight, Grace wouldn't be his type, a huge fight
    breaks out.

"Alley Cats"
Episode #119, Original Air Date 4/22/1999
By Jhoni Marchinko & Alex Herschlag
Directed by James Burrows
Rob and Ellen decide Grace is too competitive and no
    longer want to play games with her. Grace is offended
    that they don't hold Will accountable for his own
    competitive streak. When the group goes bowling,
    Grace plays terribly to bring out the competition
    in Will.

"Yours, Mine or Ours"
Episode #120, Original Air Date 3/2/1999
Written by Ellen Idelson and Rob Lotterstein
Directed by James Burrows
When a new cute guy moves into the building, both
    Will and Grace compete for his affections, not know-
    ing if he prefers boys or girls.

"Saving Grace"
Episode #121, Original Air Date 4/29/1999
Written by Jhoni Marchinko
Directed by James Burrows
Will agrees to go out with the horribly obnoxious
    publicist to the stars, Nathan Barry, so that he'll hire
    Grace to design his apartment.

"Object of My Rejection"
Episode #122, Original Air Date 5/13/1999
Written by Adam Barr
Directed by James Burrows
After Will and Grace get into a fight over her ex Danny's
    return, Will realizes he is overly invested in Grace's
    love life. The two decide that living together is pre-
    venting them from moving on to new relationships.
    Meanwhile Jack and Rosario get hitched so Rosario
    can legally stay in the country.

FAVORITE MOMENTS OF
WILL & GRACE

"My favorite episode is the pilot. I remember every-thing that went into it. Over the course of the first few weeks everything just gelled."

—David Kohan, Series Co-Creator

"My favorite line is from the episode where Karen's liv-ing in her limo ["Boardroom and a Parked Place"]. Grace is spooning Karen and Karen says, 'Grace, that had better be your penis I feel.'"

—Jon Kinnally, Writer and Executive Producer

"My favorite line is from the gay spelling bee episode ["A Story, Bee Story"]. Jack needs to hear Karen use 'Doily' in a sentence when they are sitting at the Jacques café. She says, 'He went doily down the street.' I still laugh when I think about it."

—Tracy Poust, Writer and Executive Producer

"There were many favorite behind-the-scene moments with the cast and writers. One time there was a grand piano on the set. Harry Connick, Jr., was also guest-starring that week. When the stage manager called a fifteen-minute break, everyone left the stage and went off to their rooms. I watched Harry wander over to the piano and start running his fingers over the keys. I pulled a chair up while he played a perfect rendition of 'Our Love Is Here to Stay.' I felt like the luckiest person in the world to be watching this extraordinary moment up close. There were a lot of magical moments like that on the set of *Will & Grace*."

—Tim Bagley ("Larry")

"My favorite moment was in the Jennifer Lopez episode ["I Do. Oh, No, You Di-in't"]. Jack was offering a shrimp to Rosario, saying, 'Shrimp?' And I'm walking by thinking he's calling me a shrimp, so I say, 'Queer!' It was just a last-minute change and looks like an ad lib, but it wasn't. My favorite moment off-camera was in the final episode. I had to fly out the window and they had gotten this $4,000 velvet smoking jacket from England with this paisley silk interior—it was gorgeous—and these velvet opera slippers. They had to cut the back of the jacket to put a harness on me. The crew was to pull this lever and I would fly up into the air like Peter Pan. It was just a blast. Later, when we got in front of the audience, I don't know if they pulled the lever too hard, but I went out so fast that I flew out of my shoes. All that was left of Beverly Leslie was two little opera slippers. I was so sad they didn't catch it on camera."

—Leslie Jordan ("Beverly Leslie")

FAVORITE LINES FROM SEASON 1

GRACE: "Look at the size of this place. My hair doesn't even fit in here."

JACK: "This week, Joey teaches Blossom a valuable lesson about tough love."

WILL TO JACK: "Whenever you open your mouth, a purse falls out."

KAREN: "Bacne? Oh, who am I kidding? It's alabaster from my neck to my ass."

Season 2

"Guess Who's Not Coming to Dinner"
Episode #201, Original Air Date 9/21/1999
Written by David Kohan & Max Mutchnick
Directed by James Burrows
Grace moves across the hall but still spends most of her
    time at Will's. When Will blows up at her, Grace
    decides to have a dinner party without Will at her
    apartment.

"Election"
Episode #202, Original Air Date 9/28/1999
Written by Adam Barr

QUOTE

WILL: "It's just when you moved in, it was so we could heal and then move on."
GRACE: "I know and I don't feel like I've moved on. Have you?"
WILL: "I'm standing here making out with a girl. That's the international symbol for not moving on."

Directed by James Burrows
Will and Grace both run for president of their tenants' association. Meanwhile, Karen thinks Jack's parrot Guapo has escaped on her watch. To make it up to him, she showers Jack with gifts. Eventually Jack admits Guapo returned and he's been mooching.

"I Never Promised You an Olive Garden"
Episode #203, Original Air Date 12/14/1999
Written by Tracy Poust & Jon Kinnally
Directed by James Burrows
Will and Grace ditch longtime friends Rob and Ellen for

a more exciting, hipster couple: Naomi and Kai. The new friends turn out to be too cool for Will and Grace, who retreat back into the arms of the Olive Garden–loving Rob and Ellen.

"Polk Defeats Truman"
Episode #204, Original Air Date 11/16/1999
Written by Jeff Greenstein
Directed by James Burrows
When Harlin decides to buy a cable company, Will drops all his clients so that he can exclusively focus on the soon-to-be mogul and reap the financial rewards. Sadly, Harlin changes his mind about the deal and fires Will.

"Das Boob"
Episode #205, Original Air Date 11/2/1999
Written by Jhoni Marchinko
Directed by James Burrows
An old boyfriend spots a bosomy photo of Grace in a newspaper and calls her to reconnect. Thinking he's expecting a big-boobed Grace, she goes to meet him wearing a water-filled bra that gives her what nature denied her. Sadly, the bra springs a leak.

"To Serve and Disinfect"
Episode #206, Original Air Date 11/23/1999
Written by Katie Palmer
Directed by James Burrows
Jack challenges Will to be a cater-waiter for a night when Will dismisses Jack's job as something a monkey with a tux could manage. Will agrees to serve for the night but when he runs into his old law colleagues

he panics, nearly ruining the dinner. Meanwhile, Grace learns that Karen starred in some naughty movies back in the day.

"Homo for the Holidays"
Episode #207, Original Air Date 11/25/1999
Written by Alex Herschlag
Directed by James Burrows
Will invites Jack's mother for a Thanksgiving dinner at his house. Once Jack's mother arrives the gang learns that Jack still hasn't come out to her. When Jack does finally leave the closet, his mother is supportive and reveals a secret of her own: Jack's real father is a stranger she slept with at a party and never saw again.

"Whose Mom Is It, Anyway?"
Episode #208, Original Air Date 11/9/1999
Written by Alex Herschlag
Directed by James Burrows
Grace is jealous when her mother fixes Will up instead of her daughter. Meanwhile Jack and Rosario must convince an INS worker that they are really married.

"He's Come Undone"
Episode #209, Original Air Date 2/8/2000
Written by Adam Barr
Directed by James Burrows
Will has sex dreams about Grace, which naturally sends him straight into therapy. When Will brings Grace to a therapy session, Grace and the therapist hit it off and date, but Grace won't sleep with him. The shrink uses Will's therapy to find a way into Grace's pants,

and Will realizes that his dreams are about Grace
needing to be the center of attention, sometimes at
Will's expense.

"Hey La, Hey La, My Ex-Boyfriend's Back"
Episode #210, Original Air Date 3/14/2000
Written by Jeff Greenstein
Directed by James Burrows
When Grace takes a job designing Michael's townhouse,
Will assumes his ex has reappeared to get back
together. When Will sees that Michael actually has a
new boyfriend now, Will realizes it's time to move on.

"Terms of Employment"
Episode #211, Original Air Date 11/30/1999
Written by David Kohan & Max Mutchnick
Directed by James Burrows
When Ben Doucette (Gregory Hines) breaks a contract
with Grace, she hires Will to claim her owed income.
Ben is impressed with Will's skills and offers him a
job at his firm, Doucette and Stein, one of the best in
New York.

"Seeds of Discontent"
Episode #212, Original Air Date 1/25/2000
Written by Jhoni Marchinko
Directed by James Burrows
Will's high-school girlfriend, Claire (Megyn Price), asks
him to donate sperm so that she may have a baby.
Grace gets angry, claiming Will's sperm is "hers." Will
accuses Grace of being selfish but before he can make
his deposit at the sperm bank, he realizes if he's ever

going to have a baby with a woman, he'd want it to be Grace.

"Oh, Dad, Poor Dad, He's Kept Me in the Closet and I'm Feeling So Sad"
Episode #213, Original Air Date 2/15/2000
Written by Katie Palmer
Directed by James Burrows
Will's father, George Truman (Sydney Pollack), asks Will not to attend a company party honoring George. Will, thinking his dad really wants him to come, decides to surprise him, but when he arrives he learns that all these years George has told his co-workers Will is straight and married to Grace. George tries to make amends by outing his son in a speech before the entire company.

"Acting Out"
Episode #214, Original Air Date 2/22/2000
Written by David Kohan & Max Mutchnick
Directed by James Burrows
Jack and Will are excited because sitcom *Along Came You* is about to feature the first-ever kiss between two gay men on network television. But when the kiss never happens, Will and Jack decide to go down to the network offices and protest. Jack and Will end up kissing on the *Today* show, giving network viewers a glimpse of a real gay kiss.

"Tea and a Total Lack of Sympathy"
Episode #215, Original Air Date 1/11/2000
Written by Tracy Poust & Jon Kinnally

Directed by James Burrows
Under Ben's orders, Will court's Karen's husband,
Stanley, as a client. Meanwhile, Jack and Grace go on
the show *Antiques on the Road*, where they learn they
are in possession of a pricey teapot.

"There But for the Grace of Grace"
Episode #216, Original Air Date 4/18/2000
Written by Michelle Spitz
Directed by James Burrows
When Will and Grace visit their beloved, retired, gay
college professor and his shrew of a best friend, they
see a disturbing picture of their possible future.

"Sweet (and Sour) Charity"
Episode #217, Original Air Date 4/04/2000
Written by Gail Lerner
Directed by James Burrows
Will and Grace volunteer at a community center where
they are assigned to direct a children's production of
Stone Soup. When the production is moved to the night
of a Joni Mitchell concert that they were planning on
attending, Grace bails, leaving Will with the kids.

"Advise and Resent"
Episode #218, Original Air Date 2/29/2000
Written by Tracy Poust & Jon Kinnally
Directed by James Burrows
Ben sets Will up on a successful blind date. Meanwhile,
Karen tells Grace to play hard to get with her new,
unassertive boyfriend, Josh (Corey Parker). When
Josh figures out that Karen was behind the strategy,

he tells Grace and Karen off. Both women are suddenly incredibly turned on.

"An Affair to Forget"
Episode #219, Original Air Date 4/18/2000
Written by Alex Herschlag & Laura Kightlinger
Directed by James Burrows
Rob and Ellen ask Will and Grace to be the Best Man and Maid of Honor at their wedding. But when Ellen finds out Grace and Rob slept together when both were single, Ellen calls the wedding off. Meanwhile, Jack is worried when he gets a "rise" from a female stripper at Rob's bachelor party. He's relieved when he discovers the stripper isn't really a woman.

"My Best Friend's Tush"
Episode #220, Original Air Date 5/23/2000
Written by Rob Lotterstein & Ellen Idelson
Directed by James Burrows
Grace is intimidated when she finds out she'll be competing with interior design legend Helena Barnes (Joan Collins) for the same job. Meanwhile Jack enlists Will's help in marketing his new invention, "the Subway Tush."

"The Hospital Show"
Episode #221, Original Air Date 3/28/2000
Written by Adam Barr
Directed by James Burrows
When Stanley has a heart attack, Will, Grace, Jack, and Rosario make a bet to see which one of them Karen will cry to first.

"Girls, Interrupted"
Episode #222, Original Air Date 5/02/2000
Written by Jhoni Marchinko and Tracy Poust & Jon
    Kinnally
Directed by James Burrows
Against her better judgment, Grace befriends her
    neighbor, the mentally unstable Val. Their
    friendship dies when Grace discovers that Val stole
    her music box that plays "Hava Nagila." Meanwhile,
    Jack and Karen crash a meeting of "Welcome Back
    Home," a group for ex-gay, married couples because

FAVORITE LINES FROM SEASON 2

KAREN: "You call me down to this godforsaken place, to tell me my kids made the honor roll?! Honey, my time is precious! Call me when one of them gives birth at the prom!"

JACK: "There are no straight men, only men who haven't met Jack."

GRACE: "Will, what is the point of having a gay best friend if you're not gonna dress me?"

WILL: "There was a time when I was a boob man. Of course, it ended when my mom switched to formula."

Jack has a crush on their leader, Bill (Neil Patrick Harris).

"Ben? Her?"
Episodes #223/#224, Original Air Date 5/23/2000
Written by David Kohan & Max Mutchnick
Directed by James Burrows
Will urges Grace to be nicer to Ben. She follows his instructions a little too well and the two start up a romance. When Will catches Ben with another woman he threatens to quit his job, only to learn that Grace and Ben agreed to see each other people. Will jets off to the Cayman Islands to work for Karen, but Ben follows and begs Will to return. Jack and Rosario's marriage falls apart and Jack moves into Will's apartment.

Season 3

"New Will City"
Episode #301, Original Air Date 10/12/2000
Written by David Kohan & Max Mutchnick
Directed by James Burrows
Will returns from the Cayman Islands and is jealous of Jack and Grace's newfound closeness.

"Fear and Clothing"
Episode #302, Original Air Date 10/19/2000
Written by Adam Barr
Directed by James Burrows
When someone tries to break into Grace's apartment,

she moves back in with Jack, switching places with Will. Meanwhile, Jack and Karen fight over Jack's divorce settlement form his marriage with Rosario.

"Girl Trouble"
Episode #303, Original Air Date 10/26/2000
Written by David Kohan & Max Mutchnick
Directed by James Burrows
Will organizes a gay sensitivity seminar for the police department. Grace hires a new intern, Gillian, who wants to be just like Grace . . . until she meets Karen.

"Swimming Pools . . . Movie Stars"
Episode #304, Original Air Date 11/9/2000
Written by Katie Palmer
Directed by James Burrows
In order to infiltrate the life of their hero, Sandra Bernhard, Will and Grace pose as home-buyers interested in her condo.

"Husbands and Trophy Wives"
Episode #305, Original Air Date 10/19/2000
Written by Kari Lizer
Directed by James Burrows
Will and Jack are disappointed when they visit their friends, former party boys Joe and Larry, who are now settled in suburbia with an adopted daughter.

"Grace 0, Jack 2000"
Episode #306, Original Air Date 11/02/2000

Written by Jon Kinnally & Tracy Poust

Jack's new show, *Jack 2000*, gets a boost in popularity when Jack decides to make fun of Will. Ben and Grace break up.

"Three's a Crowd, Six Is a Freak Show"
Episode #307, Original Air Date 12/14/2000
Written by Jhoni Marchinko
Directed by James Burrows
Grace dates six-toed Mark. Meanwhile Jack and Will discover they're both dating the same guy.

"Love Plus One"
Episode #308, Original Air Date 11/09/2000
Written by David Kohan & Max Mutchnick
Directed by James Burrows
At Banana Republic, Jack falls hard for intellectual, hunky customer Matthew (Patrick Dempsey). Jack begs Will to tell him what to say through his headset, like Cyrano de Bergerac.

"Lows in the Mid-Eighties"
Episode #309/#310, Original Air Date 11/23/2000
Written by Jeff Greenstein
Directed by James Burrows
The gang flash back to 1985, when Will and Grace were dating, Jack was the inspiration for Will to come out of the closet, Karen was a party girl with a long line of suitors, and Rosario sold cigarettes at a trendy club.

"Coffee and Commitment"
Episode #311, Original Air Date 1/04/2001

Written by Adam Barr
Directed by James Burrows
Joe and Larry's wedding in Vermont sparks an argu-
    ment between Will and Grace about Grace's
    mooching and Will's fear that people assume she's
    his wife.

"Gypsies, Tramps, and Weed"
Episode #312, Original Air Date 11/16/2000
Written by Katie Palmer
Directed by James Burrows
Will visits "Psychic Sue," who gives him the disturbing
    prediction that he will spend the rest of his life with
    Jack. Meanwhile, Jack becomes obsessed with his new
    Cher doll, but when he actually runs into the diva
    herself, he mistakes her for a drag queen.

"Crazy in Love"
Episode #313, Original Air Date 2/01/2001
Written by Tracy Poust & Jon Kinnally
Directed by James Burrows
Will, fearing sportswriter Matthew will be turned off by
    his lack of athleticism, finds himself pretending to be
    interested in sports.

"Brothers, A Love Story"
Episode #314, Original Air Date 2/08/2001
Written by David Kohan & Max Mutchnick
Directed by James Burrows
Things are great between Will and his new boyfriend,
    Matthew, until Will realizes that Matthew is in the
    closet at work.

FAVORITE LINES FROM SEASON 3

KAREN: "Good Lord. I can't believe I'm at a public pool. Why doesn't somebody just pee directly on me?"

JACK: "Sorry I called you a tight-ass cyber-sissy."
WILL: "Oh, that's OK. Sorry I called you a shallow, youth-obsessed, prancing cabaret queen."
JACK: "You didn't call me that."
WILL: "Well, I meant to."

KAREN: "You know I do have a family."
GRACE: "I know. I just always imagined they lived in pods somewhere in your boiler room ... And they only came out at night to race from village to village stealing people's essences."

Q FACT

Helena Barnes was supposed to appear in Season 3's "My Uncle the Car," where she and Karen would play billiards for ownership of Rosario. The women were to have a *Dynasty*-like catfight. Joan Collins turned the appearance down, and the role of Beverly Leslie was conceived.

"My Uncle the Car"
Episode #315, Original Air Date 2/15/2001
Written by Kari Lizer
Directed by James Burrows
After Grace sells her Uncle Larry's car to Sister Louise
    (Ellen DeGeneres), a nun with a cheesecake delivery
    business, she realizes she wants it back as a memento
    of her relative. Meanwhile, Beverly Leslie (Leslie
    Jordan) tries to steal Rosario from Karen.

"Cheaters, Part I & Cheaters, Part II"
Episodes #316 & #325, Original Air Date 2/22/2001
Written by Alex Herchlag
Directed by James Burrows
Will and Grace discover Will's father, George, is having
    an affair with a giggly mistress named Tina.

"Poker? I Don't Even Like Her"
Episode #317, Original Air Date 3/29/2001
Written by Mimi Friedman and Jeannette Collins
Directed by James Burrows
Joe, Larry, and Rob want Grace kicked out of Poker
    night. Karen considers getting shoulder implants.

"Alice Doesn't Lisp Here Anymore"
Episode #318, Original Air Date 5/03/2001
Written by Sally Bradford
Directed by James Burrows
Grace shows up at the funeral for a girl she teased in
    high school, only to realize the girl is still alive and
    still hates Grace.

"Mad Dogs and Average Men"
Episode #319, Original Air Date 3/15/2001
Written by Adam Barr
Directed by James Burrows
Will wants to break up with Paul (Peter Jacobsen) but
    sticks around for the boyfriend's dog.

"Old Fashioned Piano Party"
Episode #320, Original Air Date 4/19/2001
Written by Jhoni Marchinko, Tracy Poust, & Jon
    Kinnally
Directed by James Burrows
Grace is irrationally worried Will will move to San Fran-
    cisco and leave her, so she buys a piano, prompting
    more nights in together. Jack takes up writing erotica.

"The Young and the Tactless"
Episode #321, Original Air Date 5/03/2001
Written by Jeff Greenstein
Directed by James Burrows
Karen tricks Will and Jack into babysitting Stan's
    mother, Sylvia (Ellen Albertini Dow). She happily
    accompanies them to a hip gay club, then panics
    when she finds out she's out on the town with "fags."

"Last of the Really Odd Lovers"
Episode #322, Original Air Date 5/10/2001
Written by Kari Lizer
Directed by James Burrows
Will is embarrassed to be dating a twenty-four-year old,
    and Grace is embarrassed to be dating sloppy Nathan

Q FACT

Will enjoys his first passionate on-screen kiss in "Last of the Really Odd Lovers."

(Woody Harrelson) from 12C. Meanwhile, Val becomes Jack's new, scary groupie.

"Sons and Lovers"
Episodes #323/324, Original Air Date 1/04/2001
Written by David Kohan & Max Muchnick
Directed by James Burrows
Much to Will's dismay, Grace invites Nathan to move in with her and Will. Surprisingly, Will warms up to Nathan, while Grace suddenly gets cold feet about their relationship. Meanwhile, Jack learns his father, Joe Black, is dead, and that he has a son, Elliot (Michael Angarano), from a sperm donation he made when he was 17.

Season 4

"The Third Wheel Gets the Grace"
Episode #401, Original Air Date 9/27/2001
Written by David Kohan & Max Muchnick
Directed by James Burrows
Nathan grows jealous of the bond Grace shares with Will while Jack tries to bond with his son, Elliot, at a Barney's sale but the boy prefers shopping at Target.

"Past and Presents"
Episode #402, Original Air Date 10/04/2001
Written by Tracy Poust & Jon Kinnally
Directed by James Burrows
Kevin (Adam Goldberg), a bully from Will's past, lands
    a job at Doucette and Stein.

"Crouching Father, Hidden Husband"
Episode #403, Original Air Date 10/11/2001
Written by Adam Barr
Directed by James Burrows
Jack helps Elliot with his crush, Nancy, at the
    seventh-grade dance. The FBI questions Karen and
    Will about Stan's insider trading.

"Prison Blues"
Episode #404, Original Air Date 10/18/2001
Written by Alex Herschlag
Directed by James Burrows
Will freezes in front of a news reporter's camera, so Jack
    convinces him to attend his acting class. Grace is an
    overnight guest at Karen's mansion but overstays
    her welcome.

"Loose Lips Sink Relationships"
Episode #405, Original Air Date 10/25/2001
Written by Kari Lizer
Directed by James Burrows
Karen gives Grace and Nathan bad relationship advice.
    Meanwhile, Jack gets a new job at Barney's, where his
    crazy boss, Dorleen (Parker Posey), gets a crush
    on Will.

"The Rules of Engagement"
Episode #406, Original Air Date 11/1/2001
Written by Jeff Greenstein
Directed by James Burrows
Nathan proposes to Grace in the middle of sex. Grace
    wants Nathan to propose to her under different
    circumstances. Nathan realizes a relationship with
    Grace is too difficult.

"Bed, Bath, and Beyond"
Episode #407, Original Air Date 11/8/2001
Written by Jhoni Marchinko
Directed by James Burrows
Grace can't get out of bed after her breakup with Nathan.

"Star-Spangled Banter"
Episode #408, Original Air Date 11/15/2001
Written by Cynthia Mort
Directed by James Burrows
Will supports a gay man for city council while Grace
    supports a Jewish woman.

"Stakin' Care of Business"
Episode #409, Original Air Date 12/06/2001
Written by Bill Wrubel
Directed by James Burrows
Karen denies Grace a loan to purchase the office space next
    door to Grace Adler designs. At the gym, Will avoids
    his former rebound fling, Mitchell, aka "Cuddlebum."

"A Movable Feast"
Episodes #410/#411, Original Air Date 11/22/2001

Written by Kari Lizer

Directed by James Burrows

For Thanksgiving this year, Will, Grace, Jack, and
Karen decide they will only spend an hour at each of
their respective dysfunctional family celebrations.
After they all flee disastrous situations, everyone
runs back for an extra two minutes to make things
right.

"Whoa Nelly"

Episode #412, Original Air Date 12/21/2001

Written by Adam Barr

Directed by James Burrows

Will and Grace try to set up George's mistress, Tina,
with a man who's not married to Will's mother.
When the date Grace had lined up falls through,
Larry has to step in. Meanwhile, Karen and Jack
purchase a gay horse named Lamar.

"Jingle Balls"

Episode #413, Original Air Date 12/23/2001

Written by Laura Kightlinger

Directed by James Burrows

Will is embarrassed by his dancer boyfriend, Robert.
When Dorleen gives Jack 24 hours to redecorate his
Barney's display, Grace steps in and saves him.

"Dying Is Easy, Comedy Is Hard"

Episode #414, Original Air Date 1/31/2002

Written by Darleen Hunt

Directed by James Burrows

Will and Grace attend the wedding of Grace's ex-fiancé,

Danny. Jack gets Elliot a haircut that his mother, Bonnie (Rosie O'Donnell), deems gay.

"Someone Old, Someplace New"
Episode #415, Original Air Date 2/28/2002
Written by Darleen Hunt
Directed by James Burrows
Karen's birthday. Jack makes the biopic *The Mystery of Karen Walker*. During his research he uncovers the identity of Karen's estranged mother, Lois (Suzanne Pleshette).

"Something Borrowed, Someone's Due"
Episode #416, Original Air Date 3/07/2002
Story by Darleen Hunt and Teleplay by Adam Barr & Bill Wrubel
Directed by James Burrows
Jack reunites Karen with her con-artist mother, who drags Karen into one of her schemes. Will and Grace sublet their place to Rob and Ellen but gouge them on the rent.

"Grace in the Hole"
Episode #417, Original Air Date 1/17/2002
Written by Bill Wrubel
Directed by James Burrows
Will, Grace, and Jack visit Stan in prison. While there, Grace runs into Glenn (Kirk Baltz), a man she had a crush on in high school. Rosario challenges Jack and Karen to spend three nights in her room to understand the prison experience.

"He Shoots, They Snore"
Episode #418, Original Air Date 4/11/2002
Written by Sally Bradford
Directed by James Burrows
Grace teaches an interior design seminar but her students
    are only interested in seeing celebrities' houses. Jack
    is upset when Elliot asks Will's advice about his
    crush, Nancy.

"A Chorus Lie"
Episode #419, Original Air Date 2/07/2002
Written by Tracy Poust & Jon Kinnally
Directed by James Burrows
For the last spot in the Gay Men's Chorus, Jack com-
    petes with Owen (Matt Damon), a straight man
    pretending to be gay.

"Wedding Balls"
Episode #420, Original Air Date 4/18/2002
Written by Laura Kightlinger
Directed by James Burrows
Grace gets carried away when she helps Will's cousin's
    fiancée with wedding details. Jack is jealous when
    Karen and Will bond over reading the same book.

"Fagel Attraction"
Episode #421, Original Air Date 4/25/2002
Written by Jenji Kohan
Directed by James Burrows
When Will's laptop is stolen, Detective Hatch (Michael
    Douglass) devises a fake sting operation to bring

himself closer to his latest crush: Will! Meanwhile, crazy Val is back and this time she's going after Grace's business.

"Cheatin' Trouble Blues"
Episode #422, Original Air Date 3/28/2002
Written by Alex Herschlag
Directed by James Burrows
Will discovers that both his parents have something going on the side, and neither one wants to bring their affairs out into the open.

"Went to a Garden Party"
Episode #423, Original Air Date 4/04/2002
Story by Sally Bradford, Written by Tracy Poust & Jon Kinnally
Directed by James Burrows
Will's parents are separating and selling their house, leaving Will his favorite gnome statue, "Squatsie." Jack stars in a commercial for "Señor Mattress."

"Hocus Focus"
Episode #424, Original Air Date 5/02/2002
Written by Sally Bradford
Directed by James Burrows
Will wins a photo session with photographer to the stars Fannie Lieber (Glenn Close). Jack opens a magic show but runs into problems when his assistant, Karen, steals the spotlight.

"A Buncha White Chicks Sittin' Around Talkin'"
Episode #425, Original Air Date 5/09/2002

FAVORITE LINES FROM SEASON 4

KAREN: "You say potato, I say vodka."

BEVERLY LESLIE: "Karen Walker . . . I thought I smelled gin and regret."

JACK: "Oh, interesting. You gave me the straight-guy-double-pat-on-the-back-no-hip-contact hug."
OWEN (MATT DAMON): "Actually it was more the gay-guy-bend-at-the-waist-feel-your-delts-check-out-your-shoes hug."

Written by David Kohan & Max Mutchnick
Directed by James Burrows
Will and Grace decide to have a baby together. Karen learns Stan has been sentenced to extra prison time for continuing his insider trading from behind bars. After a bad audition, Jack gives up acting.

Q FACT

"A Buncha White Chicks Sittin' Around Talkin'" marks the last script by David Kohan and Max Mutchnick until "The Finale" in Season 8.

"A.I. Artificial Insemination" Part I & II
Episodes #426/427, Original Air Date 5/16/2002
Written by Tracy Poust & Jon Kinnally
Directed by James Burrows
Grace, on her way to the sperm bank with Will's sample
in hand, runs straight into a lamppost, and a mysteri-
ous stranger comes to her aid. Jack receives some advice
from Cher in a dream. Karen meets the suave Lionel
Banks at a bar and contemplates cheating on Stan.

Season 5

"Bacon and Eggs"
Episode #501, Original Air Date 10/03/2002
Written by Tracy Poust & Jon Kinnally
Directed by James Burrows
Grace considers going out with Leo, even though she
and Will agreed not to date anyone. Jack stalks Kevin
Bacon and accidentally winds up as his assistant.

"And the Horse He Rode In On"
Episode #502, Original Air Date 9/26/2002
Written by Tracy Poust & Jon Kinnally
Directed by James Burrows
Leo, the handsome stranger from the Season 4 finale,
pursues Grace. Karen finds it difficult to thwart
Lionel's advances.

"The Kid Stays Out of the Picture"
Episode #503, Original Air Date 10/10/2002
Written by Jhoni Marchinko

Directed by James Burrows
Grace secretly dates Leo while Will prematurely plans
  for the arrival of their baby. When Will finds out
  about Grace and Leo, he's furious. Especially when
  Grace says she wants to wait to see what happens
  with her new beau before going through with the
  insemination.

"Humongous Growth"
Episode #504, Original Air Date 10/17/2002
Written by Kari Lizer
Directed by James Burrows
After Will and Grace fight over Leo, Grace moves out.
  Jack and Karen hatch a plan to reunite them at
  Larry's daughter's birthday party.

"It's the Gay Pumpkin, Charlie Brown"
Episode #505, Original Air Date 10/31/2002
Written by Gary Janetti
Directed by James Burrows
Leo, Grace, and Will go on a pumpkin-picking bike ride.
  Jack opens Jacques, a one-table café in the hallway
  outside his apartment. Karen catches Stan having
  an affair.

"The Needle and the Omelet's Done"
Episode #506, Original Air Date 11/14/2002
Written by Tracy Poust & Jon Kinnally
Directed by James Burrows
Leo invites Grace to brunch with his "friends," but
  Grace is upset when she learns they are really his
  parents. Jack takes over Zandra's class.

FAVORITE LINES FROM SEASON 5

KAREN: "Which lever do I pull to be crushed by a safe?"

KEVIN BACON: "If I had a dollar for every time my jock strap had been stolen from the gym . . ."
JACK: "You'd have one hundred eighty-six dollars."

"Boardroom and Parked Place"
Episode #507, Original Air Date 11/07/2002
Written by Gary Janetti
Directed by James Burrows
When Stan freezes Karen's assets, she is forced to live in her limo. Will's long-absent boss, Mr. Stein (Gene Wilder), returns to the firm.

"Marry Me a Little/Marry Me a Little More"
Episodes #508/509, Original Air Date 11/21/2002

Q FACT

Will & Grace was the first prime-time sitcom to feature a wedding of a Jewish man and a Jewish woman. Their ceremony followed Jewish traditions, with Grace and Leo saying, "I do," under a chuppah.

Written by Jeff Greenstein and Bill Wrubel
Directed by James Burrows
Grace and Leo impulsively tie the knot when they run into Katie Couric conducting a mass wedding in the park for the *Today Show*. Later when they decide to have a real ceremony, Grace worries they rushed into things. Grace eventually comes around and Will walks her down the aisle, giving the bride away.

"The Honeymoon's Over"
Episode #510, Original Air Date 12/05/2002
Written by Sally Bradford
Directed by James Burrows
Karen crashes at Will's place and drives him crazy. Jack is blacklisted by the Gay Mafia.

"All About Christmas Eve"
Episode #511, Original Air Date 12/12/2002
Written by Adam Barr
Directed by James Burrows
Will resents Grace for rescinding a ticket to the *Nutcracker* when Leo is suddenly free. Jack and Karen spend Christmas Eve at Karen's swanky hotel room.

"Field of Queens"
Episode #512, Original Air Date 1/09/2003
Written by Katie Palmer
Directed by James Burrows
Will and Jack join a gay soccer league.

"Fagmalion Part One: Gay It Forward"
Episode #513, Original Air Date 1/15/2003

Written by Tracy Poust & Jon Kinnally
Directed by James Burrows
Karen fixes Will up with her newly out and schlumpy
    cousin, Barry (Dan Futterman). Jack convinces Will
    that as "senior gays," they bear the responsibility of
    helping Barry navigate gay life.

"Fagmalion Part Two: Attack of the Clones"
Episode #514, Original Air Date 1/30/2003
Written by Gary Janetti
Directed by James Burrows
Will and Jack take Barry to a gay bar. Grace picks a fight
    with Leo before he leaves to work with Doctors
    Without Borders in Africa.

"Homojo"
Episode #515, Original Air Date 2/06/2003
Written by Bill Wrubel
Directed by James Burrows
Will and Grace fear they've lost their special connec-
    tion, their "homojo." Jack meets Lorraine (Minnie
    Driver), Stan's mistress, and she's fabulous. He's torn
    between her and Karen.

"Fagmalion, Part Three: Bye, Bye Beardy"
Episode #516, Original Air Date 2/20/2003
Written by Alex Herschlag
Directed by James Burrows
Just as Will realizes he has a crush on Barry, Jack beats
    him to the punch and asks their newly beardless
    protégé to dinner.

"Women and Children First"
Episode #517, Original Air Date 2/13/2003
Written by Tracy Poust & Jon Kinnally
Directed by James Burrows
Jack runs into his old babysitter, Sissy (Demi Moore),
   and hires her to take care of him.

"Fagmalion, Part Four: The Guy Who Loved Me"
Episode #518, Original Air Date 3/13/2003
Written by Tracy Poust & Jon Kinnally
Directed by James Burrows
Both Jack and Will demand Barry pick one of them, and
   Barry chooses Will. Later, Barry tells Will he wants to
   play the field and they break up. Karen pretends to be
   a poor maid to win the heart of a studly janitor
   (Bruno Campos).

"sex, losers, and videotape"
Episode #519, Original Air Date 4/03/2003
Written by Steve Gabriel
Directed by James Burrows
Will is heartbroken over his breakup with Barry. Stein
   and Karen join Will in drowning their sorrows over
   booze. Jack helps Grace make a sex tape for Leo.

"Leo Unwrapped"
Episode #520, Original Air Date 4/17/2003
Written by Sonja Warfield
Directed by James Burrows
Will brings Leo home early to surprise Grace for her
   birthday.

"Dolls and Dolls"
Episode #521, Original Air Date 4/24/2003
Written by Kari Lizer
Directed by James Burrows
For fun, Karen wants to live like the poor, so she an-
    swers a roommate ad in a laundromat. At first, she
    bonds with her roommate, Liz (Madonna), but soon
    they hate each other.

"May Divorce Be with You"
Episode #522, Original Air Date 5/01/2003
Written by Sally Bradford
Directed by James Burrows
Will is Stan's lawyer, so Karen hires a young lawyer, J. T.
    (MaCaulay Culkin), to represent her in the divorce
    hearing. Jack subs for Karen while she's entangled in
    legal troubles.

"23"
Episode #523, Original Air Date 5/08/2003
Written by Adam Barr, Sally Bradford, Jeff Greenstein,
    Alex Herschlag, Gary Janetti
Directed by James Burrows
Stan dies unexpectedly. Will conducts the reading of
    Stan's will right after the funeral service. Lorraine is
    upset when she finds out Stan didn't leave her a dime.

"24"
Episode #524, Original Air Date 5/15/2003
Written by Gail Lerner, Kari Lizer, Jhoni Marchinko,
    Tracy Poust & Jon Kinnally, Bill Wrubel
Directed by James Burrows

Everyone deals with the aftermath of Stan's death . . . on a boat! Grace worries that Leo will have an affair with Dr. Morty (Nicollette Sheridan), the hot doctor he will be stationed with in Guatemala.

Season 6

"Dames at Sea"
Episode #601, Original Air Date 9/25/2003
Written by Adam Barr
Directed by James Burrows
Will and Jack panic when they think they've slept together after a night of drinking. Leo realizes he doesn't want to leave Grace again, so he doesn't go to Guatemala.

"Last Ex to Brooklyn"
Episode #602, Original Air Date 10/02/2003
Written by Alex Herschlag
Directed by James Burrows
When Leo invites his ex-girlfriend, Diane, to Grace's dinner party, everyone is shocked to learn she was the first (and last) woman Will slept with.

"Home Court Disadvantage"
Episode #603, Original Air Date 9/25/2003
Written by Jhoni Marchinko
Directed by James Burrows
A despondent Marilyn moves in with Will. Karen, Grace, Leo, and Beverly Leslie play doubles tennis.

"Me and Mr. Jones"
Episode #604, Original Air Date 10/23/2003
Written by Gary Janetti
Directed by James Burrows
James Earl Jones signs up for the McFarland Method.
    Jack tries to teach him to talk in a higher voice.

"Heart Like a Wheelchair"
Episode #605, Original Air Date 11/06/2003
Written by Tracy Poust & Jon Kinnally
Directed by James Burrows
Will meets the hunky Tom (Dylan McDermott) in the
    park while both men wheel their injured mothers.
    Grace visits Leo in Cambodia. Karen thinks she's
    tracked down Lorraine but finds her father, Lyle
    (John Cleese), instead.

"Nice in White Satin"
Episode #606, Original Air Date 11/13/2003
Written by Bill Wrubel
Directed by James Burrows
Karen goes for a physical, where she encounters the
    bizarre Dr. Hershberg (Jack Black). Jack decides to
    become a nurse.

"Strangers with Candice"
Episode #607, Original Air Date 12/04/2003
Written by Sally Bradford
Directed by James Burrows
At a restaurant, Karen runs into her old nemesis, Candice
    Bergen. Enjoying acting like people they are not, Grace
    flirts with a stranger and Will flirts with a woman.

FAVORITE LINES FROM SEASON 6

LEO: "What do you mean, Will was better? He couldn't find a g-spot with Yahoo! maps."

BEBE NEUWIRTH: "It's always nice to meet fans. Especially in a public place with lots of witnesses and clearly marked exits."

JACK: "It's so romantic, taking your sacred vows in the city of water slides and titty bars."

"A-Story, Bee-Story"
Episode #608, Original Air Date 10/30/2003
Written by Gail Lerner
Directed by James Burrows

QUOTE

"A gay spelling bee? Can we do that? What happened to the policy of 'Don't ask, don't spell'?"

—Will

WORDS OF THE GAY SPELLING BEE

Flounce
Hydrangea
Set design by
Eyebrow job
D-I-R-R-R-T-Y, as in Christina Aguilera's "Dirrrty"
GQ
Disinherited
Maitre d' (of a roller disco)
DeGeneres
Taffeta
Doily, as in "He went doily down the street."
Daiquiri

"Come on, Jack. 'Daiquiri.' Visualize it. Okay, now, we're at our favorite leather bar. There's a sign in the corner, which reads, 'If you're wearing a harness, daiquiris are free from 5:00 to 6:00.' Do ya see it?"
—Karen, Jack's spelling bee coach, aka Hag # 12

Karen coaches Jack when he enters a gay spelling bee.
   Leo decides he wants to go to Cambodia and he wants Grace to join him.

"The Accidental Tsuris"
Episode #609, Original Air Date 1/15/2004
Written by Jeff Greenstein

Directed by James Burrows
Lyle Finster courts Karen. Grace's freeloading sister, Janet (Geena Davis), pays her a visit.

"Swimming from Cambodia"
Episode #610, Original Air Date 11/20/2003
Written by Sonja Warfield
Directed by James Burrows
Jack has a hard time in nursing school. Grace returns from Cambodia after she and Leo run into problems with their relationship.

"Fanilow"
Episode #611, Original Air Date 12/11/2003
Written by Kari Lizer
Directed by James Burrows
Will does whatever it takes to meet Barry Manilow, including going on a date with a gross roadie. Grace is jealous when her mother, Bobbi (Debbie Reynolds), dines with Jack.

"A Gay/December Romance"
Episode #612, Original Air Date 1/22/2004
Written by Tracy Poust & Jon Kinnally
Directed by James Burrows
Will accidentally winds up with a sugar daddy. Grace becomes obsessed with a new noodle shop.

"Ice Cream Balls"
Episode #613, Original Air Date 2/5/2004
Written by Gail Lerner
Directed by James Burrows

Jack dates Will's client, Stuart. Karen and Grace visit Leo's cabin in Vermont.

"Looking For Mr. Good Enough"
Episode #614, Original Air Date 2/19/2004
Written by Gary Janetti
Directed by James Burrows
Will feels like the odd man out when he takes a cooking class filled with couples. Karen's mother, Lois, hires Grace to redo her new apartment.

"Flip-Flop: Part One"
Episode #615, Original Air Date 2/26/2004
Written by Gail Lerner
Directed by James Burrows
Will and Grace decide to become property flippers. Jack and Stuart consider buying the apartment of Jack's former acting teacher, Zandra.

"Flip-Flop: Part Two"
Episode #616, Original Air Date 3/04/2004
Written by Alex Herschlag
Directed by James Burrows
Jack gets cold feet about moving in with Stuart. Lyle proposes to Karen and she accepts.

"East Side Story"
Episode #617, Original Air Date 3/11/2004
Written by Gail Lerner
Directed by James Burrows
Will and Grace's flipping business hits a snag when they come across the Flipping Dykes, Deirdre (Edie Falco) and Monet (Chloe Sevigny).

"Courting Disaster"
Episode #618, Original Air Date 3/18/2004
Written by Sally Bradford
Directed by James Burrows
Will and Karen end up in traffic court, but the officer
    who gave them a ticket turns out to be Vince, the guy
    Joe and Larry have been wanting to fix Will up with.

"No Sex 'n' the City"
Episode #619, Original Air Date 3/25/2004
Written by Steve Gabriel
Directed by James Burrows
Grace and Jack give Will bad dating advice that nearly
    ruins his new relationship with Vince. Karen and
    Jack are upset that *Sex and the City* is going off the air
    but are momentarily cheered up when they meet Bebe
    Neuwirth at a coffee shop.

"Fred Astaire and Ginger Chicken"
Episode #620, Original Air Date 4/01/2004
Written by Ain Gordon
Directed by James Burrows
Grace is depressed about her failing marriage. Jack gives
    Karen dance lessons for her upcoming wedding.

"I Never Cheered for My Father"
Episode #621, Original Air Date 4/08/2004
Written by Adam Barr
Directed by James Burrows
Tina and Marilyn work out a time-share arrangement
    for face time with George. In a bid for Jack's atten-
    tion, Elliot tries to join the cheerleading team.

"Speechless"
Episode #622, Original Air Date 4/22/2004
Written by Sally Bradford
Directed by James Burrows
For his upcoming nursing school graduation ceremony,
   Jack struggles with writing an acceptance speech for
   his "Most Popular" award.

"I Do. Oh, No, You Di-in't"
Episodes #623/#624, Original Air Date 4/29/2004
Part 1 Written by Jeff Greenstein and Jhoni Marchinko;
   Part 2 Written by Kari Lizer and Sonja Warfield
Directed by James Burrows
Everyone but Grace flies to Las Vegas for Karen's wed-
   ding. Jennifer Lopez performs. At the ceremony, Lyle
   reveals a controlling side of his personality. By the
   wedding toast, Karen decides she wants a divorce.
   Leo reveals he had a one-night stand in Cambodia.

Season 7

"FYI: I Hurt Too"
Episode #701, Original Air Date 9/16/2004
Written by Alex Herschlag & Dave Flebotte
Directed by James Burrows
With the support of Will, Grace leaves Leo. Jack works
   as Jennifer Lopez's backup dancer until she informs
   him she's given Jack to Janet Jackson.

"Back Up, Dancer"
Episode #702, Original Air Date 9/23/2004

Written by Tracy Poust & Jon Kinnally
Directed by James Burrows
Will feels torn between boyfriend Vince and recently
    single, depressed Grace. Janet Jackson decides she
    needs to cut a dancer. Jack must compete in a
    dance-off with Karen's ex-boyfriend, Artemus (Will
    Arnett), to stay on the troupe.

"One Gay at a Time"
Episode #703, Original Air Date 9/30/2004
Written by Sally Bradford
Directed by James Burrows
Grace crashes an AA meeting for the free doughnuts
    and compassion. Will and Jack attend a focus group

FAVORITE LINES FROM SEASON 7

KAREN: Oh, Rosie. What do you mean you forgot to
TiVo *One Life to Live?* Damn it, woman! After my
body accepts your liver, I am through with you!"

WILL ABOUT VINCE'S MOTHER: "Apparently she's
never liked any of his boyfriends. So I'm gonna take her
for a day of shopping. You know, give her a whole pretty
woman makeover. Without spending more than $100."

GRACE: "Where're you taking her shopping? Flint,
Michigan?"

THE OUT TV LINEUP

Out TV: "A real gay network that only comes on after midnight when the Korean soap operas are over." Their slogan: "Watch us . . . please."

Current Programming:
Good Morning, Lesbian
On the Fluffy Side
Gay Jeopardy
Big Gay Brother
The Price is Right . . . and Gay
Ashamed Family Feud
Pink'd, a version of MTV's *Punk'd*
Untitled M.O.W. (on Out TV, an H.O.M.O.W.), written by Grace's boyfriend, Nick

for a new gay network, Out TV. The execs like Jack's ideas so much they hire him.

"Company"
Episode #704, Original Air Date 10/07/2004
Written by Sally Bradford
Directed by James Burrows
Will and Grace have awkward interactions with a new neighbor, Ned (Stephen Tobolowsky). Jack is intimidated by his colleagues at Out TV.

"Key Party"
Episode #705, Original Air Date 10/14/2004

Jack Talk, Jack's very own talk show. When Out TV is bought by the conservative Nimbus Television Networks, the show is renamed *Talk Time USA* and Jack quits.

In Development:
Queer Factor Possible directions for the series: straight folks running from gay people; gay men competing by facing different phobias, like having to get dressed for a date without a full-length mirror or having to throw a ball in front of their fathers.
The Swan A gay version of the makeover show.
Murder He/She Wrote "A tranny and a crime-solving thing."
Token Lesbians About lesbians on the subway.
Mantown The show takes place in a town where the women are missing and the hunks are shirtless.

Written by Sonja Warfield
Directed by James Burrows
Grace nearly ruins Will's birthday when she gives Vince bad advice about Will's present.

"The Newlydreads"
Episode #706, Original Air Date 10/21/2004
Written by Katte Angelo
Directed by James Burrows
Will and Jack try to save a local gay bookstore. Grace cracks when her new clients are happy newlyweds. Karen covers for Grace and does a great job, but quits when Grace takes credit for all her work.

"Will & Grace & Vince & Nadine"
Episode #707, Original Air Date 11/04/2004
Written by Gary Janetti
Directed by James Burrows
When Vince's "Grace," Nadine (Kristin Davis), doesn't
   like Will, Will worries this could be the end of the
   relationship. Karen distracts Jack when he hires her
   as his assistant at Out TV.

"Saving Grace, Again (Part 1)"
Episode #708, Original Air Date 11/11/2004
Written by Greg Malins
Directed by James Burrows
Will wants to take Grace out of town to get her mind
   off Leo.

"Saving Grace, Again (Part 2)"
Episode #709, Original Air Date 11/18/2004
Written by Gail Lerner
Directed by James Burrows
Will and Grace depart on their road trip. Jack finds the
   next spokesman for Out TV.

"Queens for a Day"
Episode #710, Original Air Date 11/25/2004
Written by Kirk J. Rudell
Directed by James Burrows
Will, Grace, Karen, and Jack join Vince's family for
   Thanksgiving.

"Christmas Break"
Episode #711, Original Air Date 12/09/2004

Written by Bill Wrubel
Directed by James Burrows
Grace breaks one of Marilyn's valuable Lladro figu-
   rines. Olivia, Karen's now teenaged stepdaughter,
   bonds with Jack, making Karen surprisingly jealous.

"Board Games"
Episode #712, Original Air Date 1/06/2005
Written by Sally Bradford
Directed by James Burrows
Scott Woolley, an adversary of Karen's from their high
   school days, tries to take over Walker, Inc.

"Partners"
Episode #713, Original Air Date 1/13/2005
Written by Alex Herschlag
Directed by James Burrows
Margot, Will's new boss, invites him to a dinner party
   where she will announce if he made partner at the
   firm. Will is embarrassed by the recently unemployed
   and depressed Vince.

"Bully Woolley"
Episode #714, Original Air Date 2/03/2005
Written by Greg Malins
Directed by James Burrows
Scott Woolley gets Grace caught up in his scheme to
   ruin Karen's life. Jack and Will meet Patti LuPone.

"Dance Cards and Greeting Cards"
Episode #715, Original Air Date 2/10/2005
Written by Gail Lerner

Directed by James Burrows

Will and Jack cause a stir when they share a spotlight dance at Karen's club's Valentine's Day gala. Working late at her office, Grace meets Nick, a dashing greeting-card writer.

"The Birds and the Bees"
Episode #716, Original Air Date 2/17/2005
Written by Steve Gabriel
Directed by James Burrows
Grace makes Will chaperone her date so she doesn't get too slutty with Nick. Karen sets Jack up with a Hot Gay Nerd (Luke Perry).

"The Fabulous Baker Boy"
Episode #717, Original Air Date 2/24/2005
Written by Kate Angelo
Directed by James Burrows
Karen's pansexual pastry chef, Edward (Stewart Townsend), has sex with Will, Karen, and Rosario.

"Sour Balls"
Episode #718, Original Air Date 3/17/2005
Written by Laura Kightlinger
Directed by James Burrows
Will and Jack mistakenly think they are buying a vacation home in an up-and-coming gay area.

"The Blonde Leading the Blind"
Episode #719, Original Air Date 4/21/2005
Written by Sonja Warfield
Directed by James Burrows

Will and Grace compete for the affections of stern
    therapist Dr. Georgia Keller (Sharon Stone).

"It's a Dad, Dad, Dad, Dad World"
Episode #720, Original Air Date 5/05/2005
Written by Jordana Arkin
Directed by James Burrows
Grace confronts her father about making her the butt of
    his jokes. Jack and Will unwittingly participate in
    Out TV's prank show, *Pink'd*.

"From Queer to Eternity"
Episode #721, Original Air Date 5/10/2005
Written by Barry Langer
Directed by James Burrows
Grace writes her will. Will quits his job to become a
    writer. Karen and Jack discover an imposter teaching
    the McFarland Method.

"Friends with Benefits"
Episode #722, Original Air Date 5/19/2005
Written by Tracy Poust & Jon Kinnally
Directed by James Burrows
Malcolm (Alec Baldwin) pretends to be a fan of Will's
    writing before recruiting him for a mysterious
    position at his company. Grace reconnects with a
    married old flame, Tom (Eric Stoltz). Jack struggles
    with a has-been, former child star.

"Kiss and Tell"
Episode #723, Original Air Date 5/19/2005
Written by Gary Janetti

Directed by James Burrows
Will discovers Malcolm has been helping Stan fake his
    death all these years. Grace and Tom kiss. Jack gets
    his own talk show: *Jack Talk*.

Season 8

"Alive and Schticking"
Episode #801, Original Air Date 9/29/2005
Written by Bill Wrubel
Directed by James Burrows
In the first live show of Season 8, Grace contemplates
    having an affair with married Tom. Will tries to get
    Malcolm to tell Karen the truth about Stan. When Karen
    finds out Rosario knew that Stan was alive, she fires her.

"I Second That Emotion"
Episode #802, Original Air Date 10/06/2005
Written by Gary Janetti
Directed by James Burrows
Grace's comments on *Jack Talk* are taken out of context
    and she angers the gay community. Karen dates
    Malcolm.

"The Old Man and the Sea"
Episode #803, Original Air Date 10/13/2005
Written by Gary Malins
Directed by James Burrows
Jack teaches Will how to swim. Malcolm and Karen
    invite Grace to double with them and Malcolm's
    friend, Dale (Andy Richter).

FAVORITE LINES FROM SEASON 8

WILL TO JACK: "You and Beverley Leslie. I think we've actually found someone you're too butch for."

KAREN: "Oh, there they are. The Jewish woman and the black man who are about to get married. I get such a kick that that's legal."

GRACE ABOUT JAMES (TAYE DIGGS): "You're sure you want me to do this? Okay. He lied about his mother's death for muffins. He abandoned his physically disabled boyfriend. But, seriously. You are never gonna get a hotter guy than that."

WILL: "He also said, 'How are we gonna shake the knocked-up redhead?'"

GRACE: "Back to Canada, baldie."

"Steams Like Old Times"
Episode #804, Original Air Date 10/20/2005
Written by Gary Malins
Directed by James Burrows
Will invites Clyde (Richard Chamberlain), an old
    gay man, to game night. When Karen learns Stan
    isn't fighting for her, she runs back to her husband.

THE LIVE SHOWS

"We wanted to do something special. It was a really fun way to catch the audience up on what had happened in the Season 7 finale. We could have Alec Baldwin explaining it all to Will in the hallway. It was challenging especially because of the time factor. *Will & Grace* episodes tended to need cutting because our actors were so funny that the laugh spread was so long. Because the first live episode ["Alive and Schticking"] was such a ratings success, the network wanted to do another one. We were like 'no way.' But then Kevin Riley [president of NBC] called and we said 'Okay!'"
—Tracy Poust, Writer and Executive Producer

"We did a live show for America. We did it twice—one for the East Coast and one three hours later for the West Coast. There was a huge food fight and a bathroom brawl scene and a whole pill gag where we opened Karen's medicine cupboard and hundreds of pill bottles

"The Hole Truth"
Episode #805, Original Air Date 11/3/2005
Written by Sally Bradford
Directed by James Burrows
Karen tries to pawn Malcolm off on Grace. Jack is upset when no one bids on him at Will's celebrity auction and carnival.

came out. It worked fine the first time, but it all went wrong the second. Sean and Debra were never good at keeping a straight face, and the audience love that. When the pills didn't come out, Megan got down on her knees and chanted and begged them to come out. I broke character and said: 'They can make King Kong, but we can't get some pills to come out of a cupboard.'"

—Eric McCormack in a 2007 interview
with the British newspaper *Metro*

"When Will opened up a cabinet and the pills were supposed to fall out but they didn't, everyone scrambled to get it open. Those episodes got the adrenaline going."

—Jon Kinnally, Writer and Executive Producer

"The nights we did those live episodes were really terrifying. You think, 'Oh no, if I mess up!' It's pretty scary when you think about it."

—Leslie Jordan ("Beverly Leslie")

"Love Is in the Airplane"
Episode #806, Original Air Date 11/10/2005
Written by Tracy Poust & Jon Kinnally
Directed by James Burrows
On a red-eye flight to London, Grace bumps into Leo
  and the two have sex. In New York, Jack tries to
  reunite Karen and Rosario.

"Birds of a Feather Boa"
Episode #807, Original Air Date 11/17/2005
Written by Abraham Higginbotham
Directed by James Burrows
Will and Jack rally behind two gay penguins. Karen and
    Grace attend Beverly Leslie's wife's memorial.

"Swish Out of Water"
Episode #808, Original Air Date 11/24/2005
Written by Kirk Rudell
Directed by James Burrows
Jack helps Grace deal with her mother, Bobbi. Will
    works for the Coalition for Justice, which targets
    slumlords . . . like Karen.

"A Little Christmas Queer"
Episode #809, Original Air Date 12/08/2005
Written by Jamie Rohnheimer
Directed by James Burrows
Grace and Sam, Will's brother, make out. Jack helps
    Jordie, Will's nephew, stage a Christmas show.

"Von Trapped"
Episode #810, Original Air Date 1/05/2006
Written by Gail Lerner
Directed by James Burrows
The gang attends a *Sound of Music* singalong. Will goes
    to the wrong theater and meets dreamboat James
    (Taye Diggs).

"Bathroom Humor"
Episode #811, Original Air Date 1/12/2006

Written by Greg Malins
Directed by James Burrows
In the second live show of Season 8, Will, Grace, and
    Jack end up stranded in the bathroom at Karen's
    swanky party.

"Forbidden Fruit"
Episode #812, Original Air Date 1/19/2006
Written by Janis Hirsch
Directed by James Burrows
Will quits the Coalition for Justice and returns to
    Doucette and Stein. Jack discovers Karen has a secret
    room in her mansion: a nursery.

"Cop to It"
Episode #813, Original Air Date 1/26/2006
Written by Sally Bradford
Directed by James Burrows
At dinner with Rob and Ellen, Grace and Will spot
    Vince working undercover as a waiter.

"I Love L. Gay"
Episode #814, Original Air Date 2/02/2006
Written by Steve Gabriel
Directed by James Burrows
Will, Karen, Jack, and Grace accompany Elliot to Los
    Angeles for a college interview. Will runs into James
    at the hotel, and they pick up where they left off.

"The Definition of Marriage"
Episode #815, Original Air Date 2/09/2006
Written by Abraham Higginbotham

Directed by James Burrows
Grace agrees to marry James so he won't be deported
  back to Canada. Grace learns she's pregnant.

"Grace Expectations"
Episode #816, Original Air Date 3/16/2006
Written by Janis Hirsch
Directed by James Burrows
Will learns that new boyfriend James is actually a
  horrible person. They break up and Grace's marriage
  to him is annulled. Meanwhile, Grace decides to tell
  Leo about the baby but his news about his upcoming
  marriage convinces her to keep quiet.

"Cowboys and Iranians"
Episode #817, Original Air Date 3/23/2006
Written by Robia Rashid
Directed by James Burrows
Jack makes Will accompany him to a gay cowboy bar.
  Grace hires a second assistant, Pam (Shohreh Agh-
  dashloo).

"Buy Buy Baby"
Episode #818, Original Air Date 3/30/2006
Written by Kirk Rudell
Directed by James Burrows
A mega-corporation takes over Out TV, changing *Jack
  Talk* into a platform for conservative new co-host,
  Amber-Louise (Britney Spears). Karen pays a
  woman, Cricket (Wanda Sykes), to have a baby
  for her.

"Blanket Apology"
Episode #819, Original Air Date 4/06/2006
Written by James Lecesne
Directed by James Burrows
Will is upset when George gives Grace Will's baby
    blanket for her baby. Father and son fight, and
    George confesses he wishes Will weren't gay. Will
    stops talking to George, who passes away days later.

"The Mourning Son"
Episode #820, Original Air Date 4/27/2006
Written by Jamie Rhonheimer
Directed by James Burrows
Everyone attends George's funeral, including Vince.
    Will realizes they belong together.

"Partners 'n Crime"
Episode #821, Original Air Date 5/04/2006
Written by Josh Silberman & Zack Slovinsky
Directed by James Burrows

WILL: Okay. Answer me this. If you're in Rome, raising this baby with Leo . . . Where am I?
GRACE: I don't know.

SOME OF THE MANY AWARDS . . .

Directors Guild of America, USA
Outstanding Directorial Achievement in Comedy
  Series
James Burrows
Years Won: 2001
Years Nominated: 1999, 2000, 2002, 2003, 2004, 2006

Emmy
Outstanding Comedy Series
Years Won: 2000
Years Nominated: 2001, 2002, 2003, 2004, 2005
Outstanding Writing for a Comedy Series
Nominated: Jeff Greenstein (2001)
Outstanding Directing for a Comedy Series
James Burrows
Years Nominated: 1999, 2000, 2001, 2002, 2003, 2005
Outstanding Lead Actor in a Comedy Series
Eric McCormack
Years Won: 2001
Years Nominated: 2000, 2003, 2005
Outstanding Lead Actress in a Comedy Series
Debra Messing
Years Won: 2003
Years Nominated: 2000, 2001, 2002, 2006
Outstanding Supporting Actor in a Comedy Series
Sean Hayes
Years Won: 2000
Years Nominated: 2001, 2002, 2003, 2004, 2005, 2006

Outstanding Supporting Actress in a Comedy Series
Megan Mullally
Years Won: 2000, 2006
Years Nominated: 2001, 2002, 2003, 2004, 2005
Outstanding Guest Actor in a Comedy Series
Won: Gene Wilder (2003), Bobby Cannavale (2005), Leslie Jordan (2006)
Nominated: Michael Douglas (2002), John Cleese (2004), Alec Baldwin (2005), Jeff Goldblum (2005), Victor Garber (2005)
Outstanding Guest Actress in a Comedy Series
Nominated: Debbie Reynolds (2000), Glenn Close (2002), Eileen Brennan (2004), Blythe Danner (2005)
Outstanding Casting for a Comedy Series
Tracy Lilienfield
Years Nominated: 2000, 2001, 2002, 2003, 2005
Outstanding Costumes for a Series
Lori Eskowitz and Mary Walbridge
Years Nominated: 2001, 2002

GLAAD Media Awards
Outstanding Comedy Series
Years Won: 1999, 2000, 2001, 2002, 2003, 2005, 2006
Years Nominated: 2004

Golden Globes
Best Television Series–Musical or Comedy
Years Nominated: 2000, 2001, 2002, 2003, 2004, 2005
Sean Hayes
Best Performance by an Actor in a Supporting Role in a Series, Mini-Series, or Motion Picture Made for Television

Years Nominated: 2000, 2001, 2002, 2003, 2004, 2005
Debra Messing
Best Performance by an Actress in a Television
   Series–Musical or Comedy
Years Nominated: 2000, 2001, 2002, 2003, 2004, 2005
Eric McCormack
Best Performance by an Actor in a Television Series–
   Musical or Comedy
Years Nominated: 2000, 2001, 2002, 2003, 2004
Megan Mullally
Best Performance by an Actress in a Supporting Role
   in a Series, Mini-Series, or Motion Picture Made for
   Television
Years Nominated: 2001, 2002, 2003, 2004

Producers Guild Award
Television Producer of the Year Award in Episodic
Years Nominated: 2001, 2002, 2003, 2004, 2005

People's Choice Award, USA
2005, Favorite Television Comedy (won)
1999, Favorite Television New Comedy Series (won)

Screen Actors Guild Award
2007, Megan Mullally, Outstanding Performance by a
   Female Actor in a Comedy Series Years Nominated:
   2006
Sean Hayes
Outstanding Performance by a Male Actor in a Com-
   edy Series
Years Won: 2006

TV Guide Award
2001:
Debra Messing, Actress of the Year in a Comedy Series
(won)
Sean Hayes, Supporting Actor of the Year in a Comedy
Series (won)
Eric McCormack, Actor of the Year in a Comedy Se-
ries (nomination)
Megan Mullally, Supporting Actress of the Year in a
Comedy Series (nomination)

Writers Guild of America Award (Episodic Comedy)
2001: Jeff Greenstein for "Hey La, Hey La, My Ex-
Boyfriend's Back" (nomination)

Will and Grace attend childbirth classes. Jack is too
busy with his new television role to support Karen in
her rocky marriage.

"Whatever Happened to Baby Gin?"
Episode #822, Original Air Date 5/11/2006
Written by Gary Janetti & Tracy Poust & Jon Kinnally
Directed by James Burrows
Will shocks Grace when he chooses raising a baby with
her over living with Vince. Grace upsets Will when
she wants to go to Rome to try to make it work with
Leo. Gin (Bernadette Peters), Karen's estranged
sister, shows up.

"We shot the final episode over four or five days. And Debra was falling apart. She was the only one who cried the whole entire week."

—Leslie Jordan "Beverly Leslie"

"The Finale"
Episodes #823/#824, Original Air Date 5/18/2006
Written by David Kohan & Max Mutchnick
Directed by James Burrows
When Leo suddenly confesses his love for Grace, she decides to break her agreement with Will and go with her ex-husband to Rome. Will and Grace don't talk for two years, in which time Grace gives birth to Lila and Vince and Will adopt a son, Ben. Karen, and Jack try to reunite Will and Grace, but their efforts fail. Years later Lila and Ben live across the hall from each other at college (just like Will and Grace back in the day), sparking a reunion between Will and Grace that mends their friendship. Lila and Ben marry. Meanwhile over the last 20 years, Karen lost all her money and Jack got out of serving as Beverly Leslie's concubine when the little guy blew off a balcony, leaving Jack a millionaire. Jack, Karen, and Rosario live together.

Final Thoughts

"When we created the show, the rooting interest was for Will and Grace to be together. That's the big cheat. In the pilot he's basically saying, 'Don't marry him. You need someone like me.' We wanted to give them both satisfying endings."

—David Kohan, Series Co-Creator

"When you're 35, problems that are cute aren't so cute at 40."

—Jon Kinnally, Executive Producer

"We thought, 'Our characters were getting older. Let's let them find love.'"

—Tracy Poust, Executive Producer

"My manager called and said, 'They're going to use you in the finale.' And I thought, 'Well they've had Cher, Madonna, Elton John . . . all these huge guests—who else are they going to have in the finale? The Pope? Barbara Streisand?' And my manager said, 'No, they just wanted family. The four, Rosario, and you.' I just burst into tears. Being an openly gay actor, I've done every sitcom known to man, and I've done some good ones. I could maybe have had Emmy nominations in the past, but for it to happen for a show that I feel has made a difference, it just meant so much. When the show first started, these great big heterosexual guys would come up to me and say, 'My girlfriend watches that show.' They would never say, 'I watch it.' By the end of the run there were perfectly heterosexual men coming up to me and saying, 'I love that show! You are so funny on that show!' I noticed the progress."

—Leslie Jordan ("Beverly Leslie")

"It was the funniest show I ever did. It got funnier as it went along. The show is a fairy tale. It is a fantasy. The characters are larger than life. We could get away with lines that we couldn't get away with anywhere else."

—James Burrows, Series Director

Answers: Q Quiz
How Good Is Your
Will & Grace
Pyramid?

1. Will's one-night stand on Fire Island
   b. Latin Things

2. Grace's Aunt Honey's stomach
   c. Things that are stapled

3. Professor Gopnick's teeth
   a. Things that are yellow

4. Will can't stand him
   b. Dennis Miller

5. The postcard Will Sent Grace from Italy or "Everybody Hurts" by R.E.M.
   c. Things that make you cry

6. If Larry ever sees her face again, he'll shoot himself
   c. Tom Cruise

Acknowledgments

I'd like to thank David Kohan, Max Mutchnick, and the entire team behind *Will & Grace* for creating one of the most amazing shows of sitcom history.

Extra special thanks to my interviewees: David Kohan, James Burrows, Tracy Poust, Jon Kinnally, Janis Hirsch, Tracy Lillienfield, Leslie Jordan, and Tim Bagley.

Thanks to the Glen-Rayner family: Daniel, Alicia, Rosa, and Olivia.

Thanks to Romi Lassally, Brianna Smith, Madeleine Smithberg, Anna Skarbek, Brad Hooper, Ami Angelowicz, Ali Blacker, Max Bernstein, Chuck Stern, Ian Garrick, Jefferson Dutton, Jack Allison, Mike Mitchell, Mary Van Luven, Jon Massey, Alison Starr, Julia Ain-Krupa, Beth Blacklow, and Kate Torgovnick.

Thanks to my project editor, Linda Carbone.

And, last but not least, thanks to my mom, Cathy Marshall.